The Story of Amelia Earhart

75ᵗʰ Anniversary of Her Disappearance 1937-2012

**Design and colorizations
by David K Bowman, Author of LEGERDEMAIN
Text by David K Bowman
Vaga Books**

*LEGERDEMAIN published by **Saga Books, Canada**

Introduction

On a stormy day in June 1928, the Fokker tri-motor Friendship dipped down out of a leaden sky to land in the bay near Burry Port, Wales. The airship taxied through the pouring rain to a nearby buoy and cut its engines. A moment later, crewman Louis "Slim" Gordon, opened a door in the fuselage, hopped out, and moored the ship to the buoy.

At the controls of the airship was Wilmer Stultz, and in the passenger compartment was a woman, who up until that flight had been a recreational aviator and a social worker in Boston. On that rainy morning, however, she was catapulted to international celebrity. Her name was Amelia Earhart.

A few months before, the young, boyish woman with tousled hair, had been asked to an interview by George Palmer Putnam, the wealthy and powerful head of G. P. Putnam's Sons, Publishers. An athletic adventurer, writer, and promoter, Putnam had been asked by wealthy New England socialite Amy Guest, who had purchased a Fokker tri-motor aircraft from Admiral Richard Byrd, to find a woman to fly across the Atlantic in that aircraft. Initially, Mrs. Guest planned to make the flight herself, to be the first woman to fly across the Atlantic, but had been pressured out of the flight by her worried family.

A masterful promoter, George Palmer Putnam, or "GP" as he liked to be called, immediately seized upon the young Amelia Earhart at their first meeting. Earhart was tall, slim and had a remarkable physical likeness to recent aviation hero Charles Lindbergh, whose nickname was "Lucky Lindy." Putnam instantly christened her "Lady Lindy", a nickname which Earhart deplored.

When asked if she wanted to make the flight, Earhart unhesitatingly jumped for it, as she was plucky, adventurous, and ambitious. She knew an opportunity when she saw one. As she said later, "You don't turn down an opportunity like that!"

The rest was history. Immediately after the flight of the Friendship, commemorative medals were struck and sold, and the young aviatrix embarked upon a number of product endorsements.

At the same time, GP hustled his young protégée off to his luxurious estate, Rocknoll, in Rye, NY, so that she would have the privacy and peace to write an account of her famous flight. This she did, and before the end of 1928, "20 Hours, 40 Minutes" was published. To this day, it is an important historical source and a sought after collectible.

Earhart then embarked upon a lucrative and busy lecture tour to discuss her new book. Upon her return to New York, she was appointed Aviation Editor for Cosmopolitan Magazine. By then, in 1929, she was all the rage.

Dissatisfied with being just a passenger on the first transatlantic flight, Earhart determined to pilot the Atlantic Ocean herself and spent the next four years in preparing for this. Preparations were set back by a crash during a practice flight in Norfolk, Virginia in 1930, which necessitated lengthy repairs that weren't completed until 1931. Shortly after the Norfolk crash, GP obtained a divorce from his wife, Dorothy, and the following February, in 1931, he and Earhart were married in a quiet ceremony.

In the spring of 1932, the aviatrix took off from Newfoundland and successfully crossed the Atlantic in 15 hours, 18 minutes, landing in a pasture in Londonderry, Ireland. Earhart was now the first woman to successfully pilot the Atlantic.

Over the next five years, under GP's guidance, Earhart set more aviation records, participated in various aviation events, continued to tour the lecture circuit, was the spokesperson for a multitude of products, and lent her name to several businesses. One of them was a line of women's clothing, which she personally designed. Another was a high quality line of luggage that continued be manufactured for years after her disappearance.

Additionally, Earhart became actively involved in establishing commercial air routes and founding airlines. But beyond that, she was an ardent feminist, who eschewed the conventional female role and forged a new one for herself. On her passport, under "occupation", she had entered, "flyer." And whenever she was on an airfield, she habitually wore custom tailored gabardine slacks, an open throated man's sport shirt with a knotted silk scarf, and a leather-flying jacket. They became her trademarks. She was one of the most talked-about, fashionable, admired, beloved, and emulated women of the 1930s. She was an icon. Her name was a household word. Even the press referred to her more often as not as just "Amelia." Everyone knew whom they were talking about.

During her brief career, she was always thinking about the next flight, because these flights kept her in the public eye. During her preparations for the round-the-world flight, she told a friend, "I think I've only got one more good flight left in me." That remark turned out to be more prescient than Earhart could know.

The following book is the story of Amelia Earhart's remarkable life.

Table of Contents

Chapter 1

Kansas Girl

O On July 24, 1897 the remarkable life of Amelia Earhart began in Atchison, Kansas in the home of her grandfather, Alfred Gideon Otis (1827–1912), a retired federal judge, president of the Atchison Savings Bank and a prominent citizen in town. Her parents were Samuel "Edwin" Stanton Earhart (1867-1931) and Amelia "Amy" Otis Earhart (1869–1962). Judge Otis had not initially approved of the marriage, nor Edwin's efforts as a lawyer.

Amelia Earhart was named, according to family custom, after her two grandmothers (Amelia Josephine Harres and Mary Wells Patton). From a young age, Earhart, nicknamed "Meeley" and sometimes "Millie", was the neighborhood leader, while her younger sister (two years her junior), Grace Muriel Earhart (1899–1998), nicknamed "Pidge," was a dutiful follower. Although their grandmother favored a more conventional upbringing, their mother leaned the other way, dressing her girls in the then avant garde "bloomers" which Earhart liked because of the freedom

Every morning, the Earhart children set off on daily on outings to explore their neighborhood. Earhart spent long hours playing with Pidge, climbing trees, hunting rats with a rifle and "belly-slamming" her sled downhill. This love of the outdoors activity and rough play, although common with many youngsters, later caused some biographers to characterize the young Earhart as a tomboy. The girls kept "worms, moths, katydids and a tree toad in a growing collection gathered in their outings. In 1904, with the help of her uncle, she built a home-made ramp modeled after a roller coaster she had seen on a trip to St. Louis and secured the ramp to the roof of the family tool shed. Earhart's first documented flight ended with her emerging from the broken wooden box that had served as a roller coaster car, with an injured lip and torn dress, exclaiming, "Oh, Pidge, it's just like flying!"

Left, Atchison in the early 1900's; above, A Bird's Eye
View of Atchison, ca 1869.

In 1908, Edwin Earhart's job with the Rock Island Railroad led to a transfer to Des Moines, Iowa. The next year, at the age of 12, Earhart saw her first aircraft at the Iowa State Fair in Des Moines. It was an unforgettable experience in which the aircraft buzzed the spot where Amelia and her sister Muriel were walking. Muriel prudently dove for cover, while Amelia calmly stood her ground, transfixed.

The two sisters, Amelia and Muriel (she went by her middle name from her teens on), remained with their grandparents in Atchison, while their parents moved into new, smaller quarters in Des Moines. While Edwin was setting up a home in Des Moines, Earhart and her sister were home-schooled by their mother and a governess. She later reminisced that she was "exceedingly fond of reading", spending many hours in the large family library. In 1908, when the family was finally reunited in Des Moines, the Earhart children were enrolled in public school for the first time.

The family's finances subsequently improved to the point where they were able to move into a new house and even hire of two servants. However Edwin was soon realized to be an alcoholic. A few years later, he was forced to leave his job and go into treatment,. but he was never reinstated by the Rock Island Railroad. In 1912, Earhart's grandparents died, leaving a substantial estate that placed her daughter's share in trust, due to a fears about Edwin's drinking. As as part of the settlement of the estate, the Otis house, and all of its contents, were auctioned. Heartbroken, Earhart later described it as the end of her childhood.

2

Chapter 2

Searching for Her Calling

I n 1915, after a lengthy job search, Earhart's father found work as a clerk for the Great Northern Railway in St. Paul, Minnesota, where Earhart enrolled in Central High School as a junior. Edwin applied for a transfer to Springfield, Missouri later that year, but the incumbent claims officer changed his mind about at the last moment, his retirement and demanded his job back. This left Edwin with nowhere to go. Worried about another disruptive move, Amy took her children to Chicago where they stayed with friends. Earhart canvassed nearby high schools in Chicago to find the best science program. She rejected the high school nearest her home when she complained that the chemistry lab was "just like a kitchen sink." She eventually enrolled in Hyde Park High School but spent a miserable semester where a yearbook caption recorded her unhappiness, "A.E. – the girl in brown who walks alone."

Earhart attended Hyde Park High School, after graduation, attended Ogontz School, from which she did not formally graduate. This was because during a trip to Toronto during her Christmas vacation in 1917 to visit Muriel, Earhart became involved with nursing and decided to stay there, after seeing returning wounded soldiers. She received training as a nurse's aide from the Red Cross and began work with the Volunteer Aid Detachment at Spadina Military Hospital. Her duties included food preparation in the kitchen for patients with special diets and dispensing prescribed medication.

Left, view of Toronto in early 1900s; right , Spadina Military Hospital in early 1900s

Left, Ogontz graduation photo, 1917; and right, Earhart as a nurse in Toronto, 1918

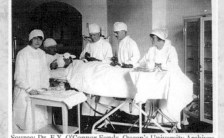

Left, a typical military hospital of the WW I period; right, typical wounded Canadian soldiers who Earhart might have helped to treat.

When the 1918 Spanish flu pandemic reached Toronto, Earhart became a patient herself, contracting pneumonia and maxillary sinusitis. She remained until early 1919. In the hospital, in a pre-antibiotic era, she had painful minor operations to wash out the affected sinus, although the procedures were not successful. Earhart subsequently suffered from worsening headache attacks, her convalescence lasting almost a year. She spent it at her sister's home in Northampton, Massachusetts, passing the time by reading poetry, learning to play the banjo and studying mechanics. Her sinus condition was to continue to affect Earhart's flying and activities in later life, and sometimes even on the airfield she was forced to wear a bandage on her cheek to cover a small drainage tube.

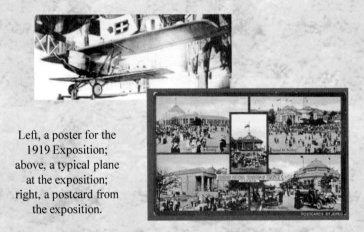

Left, a poster for the 1919 Exposition; above, a typical plane at the exposition; right, a postcard from the exposition.

At about that time, with a young woman friend, Earhart visited an air fair held in conjunction with the Canadian National Exposition in Toronto. One of the highlights of the day was a flying exhibition put on by a World War I "ace." The pilot overhead spotted Earhart and her friend, who were watching from an isolated clearing and buzzed at them. "I am sure he said to himself, 'Watch me make them scamper,'" Earhart later said. Earhart stood her ground as the aircraft came close. "I did not understand it at the time," she said, "but I believe that little red airplane said something to me as it swished by."

By 1919 Earhart prepared to enter Smith College but changed her mind and enrolled at Columbia University signing up for a course in medical studies among other programs. She quit a year later to be with her parents who had reunited in California.

4

Chapter 3

Taking Wing

I n December 1920, Earhart and her father visited an air show in Long Beach, field where noted pilot Frank Hawks, gave Earhart a ride that changed the course of her life. "By the time I had got two or three hundred feet off the ground," she said, "I knew I had to fly." After that 10-minute flight, which cost her father $10, she immediately became determined to learn to fly. Working at a variety of jobs, including photographer, truck driver, and stenographer at the local telephone company, she managed to save $1,000 for flying lessons. Earhart took her first lessons in January 1921, at Kinner Field near Long Beach. To reach the airfield Earhart took a bus to the end of the line, then walked four miles. Her mother also provided part of the $1,000 "stake" against her "better judgement." Her teacher was Anita "Neta" Snook, a pioneer female aviator who used a surplus Curtiss JN-4 "Canuck" for training. Earhart arrived with her father one day with the terse request, "My name is Amelia Earhart and I want to fly. Will you teach me?"

Earhart's commitment to learn flying meant facing the frequently hard work and rudimentary conditions that accompanied early aviation training. Her new leather jacket lacked a look of experience, so Earhart slept in it for three nights to give the jacket a "worn" look. To complete the look, she cropped her hair short in the style of other female flyers. Six months later, Earhart purchased a second-hand bright yellow Kinner Airster biplane, which she nicknamed "The Canary." On October 22, 1922, she flew the Airster to an altitude of 14,000 feet, setting a world record for female pilots. The following year, on May 15, 1923, Earhart became the 16th woman to be issued a pilot's license, #6017, by the Fédération Aéronautique Internationale (FAI).

Right, Earhart's 1923 pilot license.

Above, Earhart ca 1921 at Kinner Field

During this period, her grandmother's inheritance, which was now administered by her mother, continued to be depleted until it was wiped out after following a disastrous investment in a failed gypsum mine. As a result, with no immediate prospects for recouping her investment in flying, Earhart had to sell the "Canary" as well as a second Kinner, the proceeds from which she used to buy a yellow Kissel "Speedster" automobile, which she promptly nicknamed the "Yellow Peril." Earhart also experienced a recurrence of her old sinus problem as her pain worsened; she was hospitalized in 1924 for another sinus operation, which was again unsuccessful. After trying her hand at a number of unusual ventures including setting up a photography company, Earhart set out in a new direction. Following her parents' divorce in 1924, she drove her mother in the "Yellow Peril" on a transcontinental trip from California with stops throughout the West and even a jaunt up to Calgary, Alberta. The meandering tour eventually brought the pair to Boston, Massachusetts where Earhart underwent yet another sinus procedure, this operation being more successful. After recuperation, she returned for several months to Columbia University but was forced to abandon her studies because her mother couldn't afford the costs anymore. Eventually, she found employment first as a teacher, then as a social worker in 1925 at Denison House, setting up residence in Medford, Massachusetts.

While in Medford, Earhart continued her interest in aviation, joining the American Aeronautical Society's Boston chapter, later being elected its vice president. She flew out of Dennison Airport, which later became Naval Air Station Squantum, in Quincy, Massachusetts and helped finance its operation by investing a small amount of money. She also flew the first official flight out of Dennison Airport in 1927. As well as acting as a sales representative for Kinner airplanes in the Boston area, Earhart wrote local newspaper columns promoting flying and as her local celebrity grew, she laid out the plans for an organization devoted to female flyers.

Left, Earhart during the mid 1920s; right, at Denison House, Boston, 1926

6

Chapter 4

An Unrefusable Offer

In the spring of 1928, Captain Hilton H. Railey, a representative of publisher and publicist George Palmer Putnam, contacted Amelia Earhart and offered her the chance to fly the Atlantic aboard an airplane later dubbed the Friendship. Earhart had apparently been selected because of her activities in aviation and her altitude record. After brief skepticism, Earhart jumped at the chance, later telling interviewers that it was "an offer you don't turn down". For this flight, Earhart was to be a passenger, as well as keep the flight log. Wilmer Stultz would be the pilot and Louis Gordon his co-pilot and mechanic. The friendship took off on June 17, 1928 from Trepassey, Newfoundland after a three week wait for decent weather, landing in the harbor at Burry Port, Wales the next day. From then on, Earhart's life would never be the same: she was catapulted to instant international fame. The flight took exactly 20 hours and 40 minutes. When she was interviewed after the landing, Earhart candidly told Captain Railey, "Stultz did all the flying—had to. I was just baggage, like a sack of potatoes." She added, "...maybe someday I'll try it alone."

June 12, 1928 telegram from GP to Wilmer Stultz regarding weather and new flight path.

The Friendship off of Trepassey in June 1928

Left, Amelia Earhart and her promoter, George Palmer Putnam in Boston in 1928 before the Friendship flight.

Left, clockwise, photo of one of four different medals struck to commemorate the Friendship flight; Right, a map of Newfoundland from the period; Below left, postcard showing Boston in the period; Below center, front of a commemorative postcard of Friendship flight, from author's collection; Below right, newspaper map of Friendship flight route.

Earhart received an enthusiastic welcome on June 19, 1928, when landing at Woolston in Southampton, England. The English aristocracy immediately embraced the aviatrix, whisking her into the world of high society. She flew the Avro Avian owned by Lady Mary Heath, later purchased the aircraft, with her new found wealth and had it shipped back to the United States.

Left, a souvenir postcard of the Friendship in the harbor at Trepassey on June 28, 1928; below a memorial in the harbor at Burryport Wales; Right, a triumphant Earhart at Southampton, England after her landing at Burryport, Wales.

Colorization by David K. Bowman

8

Amelia Earhart being greeted by Mrs. Foster Welch, Mayor of Southampton, June 20, 1928.

Above, Bill Stulz, Amelia Earhart and Louis Gordon being greeted by a crowd in Southampton; Below, a period newspaper article about Earhart's stay with British nobility in 1928.

Above, left, a button issued in 1928 by the Bond Bread Co. to commemorate the flight; above right, another of the commemorative medals.

"Lindy Lady" Their Guest

While all England is enthusiastically acclaiming the feat of Amelia Earhart Putnam, the daring young aviatrix is resting as the guest of United States Ambassador Andrew W. Mellon in the English capital. As Amelia did not bring a wardrobe with her on her solo flight across the Atlantic, the important matter of feminine finery was taken care of by Mrs. David K. Bruce (left), Ambassador Mellon's daughter and official Embassy hostess. King George has expressed a desire to meet the daring flyer and it is probable that Mr. Mellon will introduce his famous countrywoman at the palace.

Above, a vintage view of Burry Port, Wales; Right, a 1928 newspaper article; Left, a relatively new coaster from a pub in Burry Port—they still remember Amelia's visit!

Left to right: Wilmer Stultz, Amelia Earhart and
a laconic Louis Gordon – Chicago Sunday
Tribune, July 15, 1928

Above left, the cover of
Earhart's first book; Above
right, the Lucky Strike ad

When the Friendship flight crew returned to the United States, they were greeted with a ticker-tape parade in New York followed by a reception with President Calvin Coolidge at the White House.

GP Putnam had noted Earhart's physical resemblance to aviator Charles Lindbergh and blatantly promoted it in the press with the nickname "Lady Lindy. The press rushed to embrace that name, making "Lady Lind a standard moniker, which Earhart loathed. More grandiloquent, the United Press referred to Earhart as the reigning "Queen of the Air". Immediately after her return to the United States, Earhart undertook an exhausting lecture tour (1928–1929). Meanwhile, Putnam had undertaken to heavily promote her in a campaign including publishing a book she authored, a series of new lecture tours and using pictures of her in mass market endorsements for products including Lucky Strike cigarettes, which caused image problems for her, resulting in *McCall's* magazine retracting a lucrative offer, and women's clothing and sportswear. The $1500 that was her share of the money from the "Lucky Strike" ad was donated to Commander Richard Byrd's imminent South Pole expedition.

One feature of photos of Earhart was her "Mona Lisa" smile, which was the result of GP's instruction to Earhart, to cover the gap between her two upper front teeth. The prim smile became one of her trademarks.

Above, left , Charles Lindbergh, and right, music for the song immortalizing AE's
resemblance to Lindbergh

Above left, Earhart, Stultz and Gordon being greeted in England, 1928; Above
center, mural on car wash in Rye, NY; Above right, a portrait of Earhart
in evening dress, ca 1929.

Shortly after her transatlantic flight, piloting Avian *7083*, Earhart embarked upon her first long solo flight. She made the trip in August 1928, becoming the first woman to fly solo across the North American continent and back. Gradually her aviation skills and professionalism grew, garnering her praise from the experienced professional pilots who flew with her. General Leigh Wade, who flew with Earhart in 1929, remarked, "She was a born flier, with a delicate touch on the stick."

Above, left, Earhart being sworn in as an honorary major in the U.S. Army Air Force, 1928;
above right, Earhart at the 1929 National Air Races in Cleveland.

Amelia Earhart wearing a favorite hat style, the cloche, circa 1930. GP didn't like the style at all on AE and urged her to wear something else, although he tried to market a version of the hat with AE's signature on it. She emphatically vetoed the idea.

Chapter 5

Becoming a Celebrity

The income from Earhart's endorsements helped finance her flying activities, which she carried on whenever she wasn't on a speaking tour. She was offered a position as associate editor at *Cosmopolitan* magazine and used her regular column to campaign for greater public acceptance of aviation, especially the participation of women entering the field. In 1929, Earhart was among the first aviators to promote commercial air travel through the development of a passenger airline service. Along with Charles Lindbergh, she represented Transcontinental Air Transport (TAT), which later became TWA. Working with Eugene Vidal, Earhart invested time and money in setting up the first regional shuttle service between New York and Washington, DC. She also helped to found National Airways, which conducted the flying operations of the Boston-Maine Airways and several other airlines in the northeast and became Northeast Airlines by 1940.

Above, first two pages of an early article by Earhart for Cosmopolitan; below left, Earhart trying deep sea diving in 1929; below right, at the 1929 National Air Races

1929 Women's Air Derby

Earhart (fourth from right,) with a group of her colleagues
at the air derby

Earhart's first attempt at competitive air racing was in 1929 during the first Santa Monica-to-Cleveland Women's Air Derby, later nicknamed the "Powder Puff Derby" by humorist Will Rogers. A telling incident occurred during the race, at the last intermediate stop before the finish in Cleveland. Earhart and her friend Ruth Nichols were tied for first place and Nichols was to take off right before Earhart. However Nichols' aircraft hit a tractor at the end of the runway and flipped over. Earhart, instead of immediately taking off, ran to the wrecked aircraft and dragged her friend out. It was only when she was sure that Nichols was uninjured that Earhart take off for Cleveland, but due to the time lost, she finished third. Earhart's courageous act was typical of her selflessness, and, just as typically, she rarely referred to the incident in later years. Earhart was a militant enough advocate for women's rights that in 1934 when legendary screen actress Mary Pickford was invited to open the Bendix Air Races in Cleveland, from which women were banned from participation, Earhart refused to fly her there for the occasion.

The large crowd in Cleveland at the finish of the first
Women's Air Derby.

14

Vera Dawn Walker during the
1929 Women's Air Derby

Louise Thaden being congratulated for her first place finish in
the 1929 Women's Air Derby.

In 1930, Earhart became an official of the National Aeronautic Association, where she actively promoted the establishment of separate women's records and was instrumental in the Fédération Aéronautique Internationale (FAI) accepting a similar international standard.

Initially, Earhart was engaged to Samuel Chapman, a chemical engineer from Boston, but broke it off on November 23, 1928. During the same period, Earhart and G.P. Putnam had been spending a lot of time together, forming a relationship. Putnam, who was known as GP, was divorced from his wife, Dorothy Binney Putnam in 1929. He began proposing frequently to Earhart, until after the sixth time, when they were married on February 7, 1931. Earhart hesitated greatly before consenting. They were married in Putnam's mother's house in Noank, Connecticut. Earhart later referred to their marriage as a "partnership" with "dual control." In a letter Earhart wrote to Putnam and hand delivered to him on the day of the wedding, she wrote, "I want you to understand I shall not hold you to any midaevil [sic] code of faithfulness to me nor shall I consider myself bound to you similarly."

Earhart's ideas on marriage were liberal for the time, as she believed in equal responsibilities for both partners and made it a point to keep her own name rather than being referred to as Mrs. Putnam. The New York Times, per its usual stylistic rules, insisted on referring to her as Mrs. Putnam, but Earhart good naturedly laughed it off. GP was soon to learn that he would be called "Mr. Earhart" by the media. Since Earhart embarked immediately upon a nine-day cross-country tour promoting autogyros for the Beechnut Gum Company, there was no honeymoon for the newlyweds. Although the union produced no children, Putnam had no children, he had two sons by his previous marriage to Dorothy Binney.

During the tour, Earhart set a world altitude record of 18,415 feet (5,613 m) in a borrowed company machine. In Abilene, Texas, the aviatrix' career nearly ended in a spectacular accident with her autogiro. During takeoff, Earhart lost control of the machine which then dropped down, hitting two parked cars. Luckily, nobody was hurt. She later told the press: "The air just went out from under me. Spectators say a whirlwind hit me. I made for the only open space available. With any other type of plane, the accident would have been more serious."

Left, a newspaper ad from the Oklahoma City Daily Oklahoman, June 1, 1931; below, graphic from same edition; above and below right, photo taken on day of Earhart's crack-up in Abilene, Texas, June 11, 1931 **(Photographer Unknown); right, a commemorative button issued by Beechnut in 1931.**

Courtesy of website of the Lincoln Highway National Museum & Archives, Galion, Ohio.

Above, Earhart flying above Pennsylvania in June 1931; Left, Earhart with her machine, during the same month, location unknown.

Earhart and Babe Didrikson shooting in 1931

Source: Kranz

Above, Amelia Earhart (L) and Florence Klingensmith, NAR, Ca. August-September, 1932

Courtesy of Iconista's Photostream

Artful 1931 Portrait of Amelia Earhart

Amelia Earhart in one of her favorite hobbies, gardening, ca 1932.

Source: Kranz

Beautiful posed portrait of Amelia Earhart circa 1931-32

Chapter 6

Proving Her Mettle --
Crossing the Atlantic Solo

Amelia Earhart at Trepassey, 20 May 1932

On the morning of May 20, 1932, a 34 year old Amelia Earhart took off from Harbour Grace, Newfoundland, carrying with her the latest copy of a local newspaper to confirm the date of the flight. The plan was to fly to Paris in her single engine Lockheed Vega 5B in emulation of Charles Lindbergh's 1927 solo flight. After a flight of 14 hours, 56 minutes during which she contended with strong winds, icy conditions, a fuel leak, and mechanical problems, Earhart landed in a pasture at Culmore, north of Derry, Northern Ireland. The landing was witnessed by Cecil King and T. Sawyer. When the first person there, Dan McCallion, asked, "Have you flown far?" Earhart replied, "From America." "Holy mother of God!" was the exclamation from the Irishman. The site now is the home of a small museum, the *Amelia Earhart Centre.*

For her flight, Earhart received the Distinguished Flying Cross from the U.S. Congress; the Cross of Knight of the Legion of Honor from the French Government; and the Gold Medal of the National Geographic Society from President Herbert Hoover. As her fame grew, she formed friendships with many people in high offices, most notably President Franklin Roosevelt and Eleanor Roosevelt (President and First Lady from 1933–1945). Eleanor Roosevelt shared many of Earhart's interests and passions, especially women's causes. After flying with Earhart, Roosevelt obtained a student permit but did not pursue her plans to learn to fly. The two friends communicated frequently throughout their lives. Another famous flyer, Jacqueline Cochran, considered Earhart's greatest rival by both media and the public, was also a confidante and friend during this period.

Above, Harbour Grace, 1911

Rare (one of 50) Atlantic Flight cover, addressed to Earhart's technical advisor Berndt Balchen

19

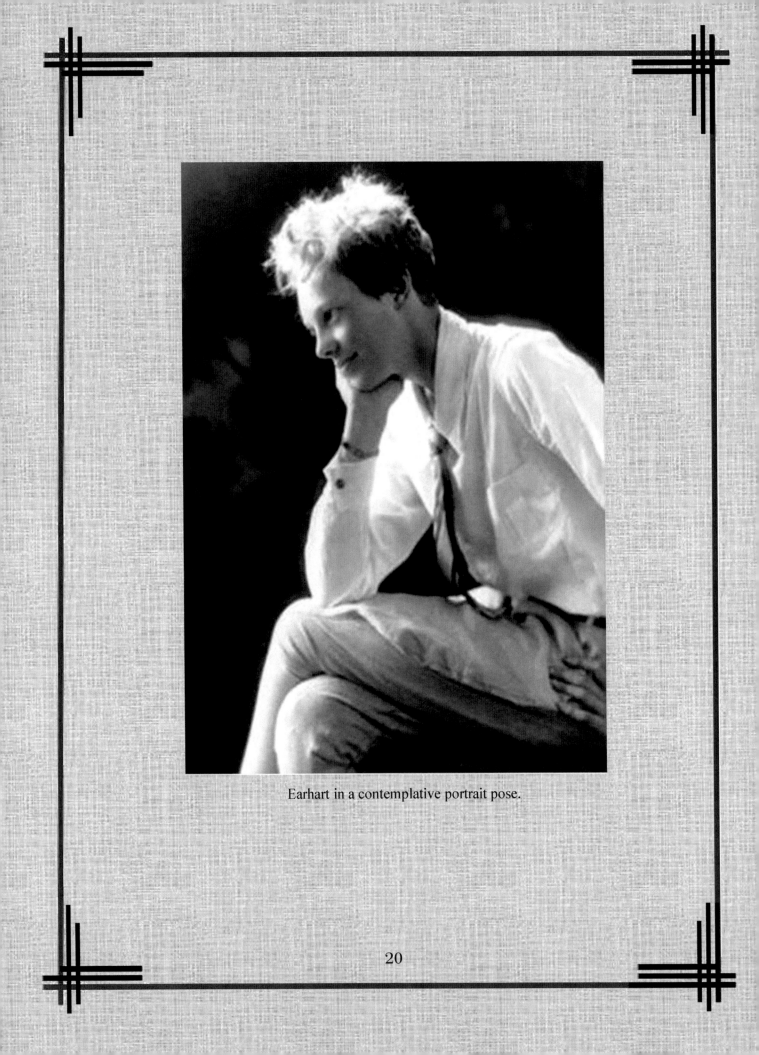

Earhart in a contemplative portrait pose.

One of the medals struck
for the 1932 flight

Staged photo taken the day
after Earhart's historic
landing at Culmore, Ireland

Earhart being feted in London,
1932

House in Culmore where Earhart stayed the night

The Lockheed Vega 5B flown by Earhart
to Ireland, now in the National Air &
Space Museum

Above left, Earhart in New York in 1932 during ticker tape parade; above right, Earhart with President Hoover in 1932; right, ticker tape parade in New York, 1932; bottom right, a nice formal portrait of Amelia Earhart, 1933; below, breathtaking view of New York City in 1932 (Manfred Curry, Verlag F. Bruckmann, München)

Chapter 7
A National Icon

A FAMOUS FLIER EXAMINES A SPEED WONDER OF THE PAST: MISS AMELIA EARHART
Takes the Throttle of the Old DeWitt Clinton, Which Originally Operated on the Mohawk Hudson Railroad a Hundred Years Ago, During a Visit to the Transportation Exhibit at the Chicago World's Fair.
(Times Wide World Photos.)

Left, Amelia Earhart at the 1933 World Fair in Chicago; Above, Earhart testing a parachute in 1935.

Amelia Earhart greeting legendary actress Mary Pickford, 1933

Source: Kranz

Autographed cover commemorating the 1933 National Air Races

HANDS of DESTINY by JOSEF RANALD

HAVE YOU THIS TRIPOID OF DARING ?

AMELIA EARHART

THE TRIPOID OF DARING —

as seen on this chart is to be found at the side of the hand underneath the first finger, denoting great courage and mental daring. Amelia Earhart was the first woman to fly over the Atlantic Ocean from west to east. She is noted for her interest in aviation.

JOSEF RANALD has analysed the hands of the world's great figures. If you want to have your own hand analysed, please send to Josef Ranald, Suite 1110, 220 East 42nd Street, New York, N. Y., for a hand chart and instructions. Inclose a self-addressed stamped envelope and 10 cents to cover clerical expense.

Copyright, 1932, by World Feature Service

Above, a fascinating 1932 news clipping from author's collection

Amelia with a 1933 Terraplane

Amelia with a 1933 Chrysler

The Hands of Amelia Earhart

Right, Nellie Simmons Meier. famed palmist, took prints of Amelia Earhart's hands in 1933 and did a character summary of her; Left, Nellie Simmons 1937 book on palmistry.

"The length of the palm indicates the love of physical activity, but the restraining influence shown by the length of the fingers, indicative of carefulness in detail, enables her to make careful preparation towards accomplishing a definite goal.

"In close joining of the life line and the head line is shown the caution which she exercises in matters of enterprise affecting herself, and with the length of the fingers before mentioned, acts as a preventative to her taking unnecessary risks or doing foolhardy stunts."

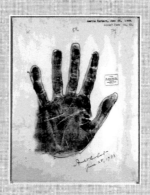

Above, left, the right handprint; to the right, left handprint of Amelia Earhart.

The character analysis of Amelia Earhart, prepared by Nellie Simmons Meier in 1933.

25

L to R, clockwise: Amelia Earhart Fashion label (Courtesy of Atlantisonnine.com); Amelia Earhart modeling one of her creations; Vintage newspaper ad for Amelia Earhart Fashions (author's collection);; vintage pages from a 1934 issue of Vogue (Courtesy of HPrint.com); Harpo and Amelia Earhart, ca 1932-34 (Courtesy of Tramontana.com)

Above, a 2009 photo of Amelia Earhart's former home
in Toluca Lake, CA

In November 1934, Earhart moved to a rented house in Toluca Lake, in North Hollywood as part of her arrangements to plan an upcoming flight. Shortly afterward, a fire broke out at the Putnam residence, Rocknoll, in Rye, New York, gutting the first floor and destroying many Putnam and Earhart family treasures and mementos. Although Putnam had already sold his interest in the New York based publishing company, Putnam &Sons, to his cousin, Palmer Putnam, he continued to maintain his residence on the East Coast because of his other business interests. This series of events marked the beginning of a quiet separation between GP and AE, in which the two basically maintained their residences on opposite coasts, due in large part to Earhart's loathing of the cold gray climate of the East. In late 1934, after her move to Toluca Lake, Earhart contacted Hollywood stunt pilot Paul Mantz to ask him to be her technical advisor on her upcoming Hawaii to Oakland flight. Mantz lived not far to her, which seemed to facilitate matters, although this later backfired on Earhart somewhat when she was named correspondent in Mantz' messy divorce in 1935. In the spring of 1935, GP did purchase a house in the Toluca Lake area and spent more time there, for various reasons including his position at Paramount Pictures.

In mid 1935 Earhart and Mantz formally established a business partnership they had been considering since late 1934 by creating Mantz Air Services, in which Mantz was given a 51 percent controlling interest. The company was located at the Burbank Airport about five miles from Earhart's Toluca Lake home.

Left, Paul Mantz after test flying Amelia Earhart's Vega in Hawaii in January 1935 (from author's collection); right, Earhart waiting before takeoff from Wheeler Field, Hawaii, January 1935.

Chapter 8

Year of Accomplishment

On January 11, 1935, Earhart made a record-setting solo from Wheeler Field in Honolulu, Hawaii to Oakland, California. This flight had been attempted by many others, most memorably by the participants in the ill-fated 1927 Dole Air Race, which was to fly from Oakland to Honolulu. Of the eight planes that started, only two reached Honolulu, with one participant turning back due to engine trouble and the rest perishing at sea. Earhart's flight was uneventful with no significant problems. However, the Sugar Growers Association of Hawaii, who were the sponsors of the flight, got cold feet due to the cost and ethical questions and the flight almost never happened. Earhart confronted them in a banquet room at the Royal Hawaiian Hotel and dissuaded them from aborting the flight.

"Gentlemen, I can sense an aroma of cowardice in this room," she began in a memorable speech that was, ironically almost in private. "I have no idea where the rumors of my political influence started," she continued. "It is inexplicable to me that you gentlemen would accept such a stupid rumor as gospel truth without giving me a chance to deny it, as I most emphatically do. My business is flying. I have spent nearly half of the sum you promised me to get my plane in condition to bring it here, but I can soon recoup that loss. I intend to fly to California within this week, with or without your support."

Above, is Earhart's arrival in Oakland at the end of her flight from Wheeler Field. Left, a monument to Earhart's 1935 flight, erected near Hanauma Bay on Oahu. Above, right, Banyan Drive, in Hilo, on the Island of Hawaii, where numerous celebrities have planted Banyan trees. Earhart planted one there on January 6, 1935, lower right, the tree Earhart planted.

Earhart and her husband in Oakland at
about the time of her Mexico flight**

O n April 19, 1935, Earhart made another record-setting flight from Los Angeles to Mexico City. To commemorate the occasion, the Mexican government issued a 20 cent Mexican airmail stamp overprinted with "Amelia Earhart/vuelo/de bueno voluntad/Mexico/1935." This translated to "Amelia Earhart, Good Will Flight, Mexico, 1935." Unfortunately, only several hundred were printed, two thirds of which were secured by G. P. Putnam. The philatelic world was not pleased when they learned how few of the stamps would be available to collectors. The 1935 overprint is now a highly sought, expensive philatelic item.

Big Reception For Aviatrix in Mexican Capital

Above, enlargement of stamp issued with commemorative overprint by Mexican government. Very rare (there are only a few hundred in available to collectors, and now worth $1200-1500 or more each. Beware of counterfeits!

Above, Amelia Earhart with a Mexican military officer during her visit to Mexico; right, a newspaper clipping of the time, reporting Earhart's arrival in Mexico City.

Unique cover mailed to G.P. Putnam from Mexico with one of the rare 1935 overprint stamps on it.

**Colorization by David K. Bowman

29

The next record attempt was a nonstop flight from Mexico City to New York. At the conclusion of her visit, at which she was joined by her husband, GP, she took off on May 8 for Newark, New Jersey, setting another record. Although her flight was uneventful, she had to contend with large crowds after landing and was concerned about taxiing too close to them.

On 2,100-Mile Nonstop Flight to New York

Amelia Earhart (above) one of America's leading women fliers, took off from Mexico City early Wednesday on a perilous 2,100-mile nonstop flight to New York City. Her monoplane loaded down with 1,000 pounds of gasoline and oil, taxied two miles along a specially constructed runway before getting into the air. Her route crosses mountain ranges two miles high.

Above, a cover carried by Amelia Earhart on her flight from Los Angeles to Mexico City and Mexico City to Newark, NJ.; left, the logo for the 1935 National Air Races

Due to an earlier ban on female pilots in the Bendix Trophy Race, which was part of the National Air Races, Earhart was the first woman pilot to participate in that race in 1935, placing fifth. It was the best she could manage given that her stock Lockheed Vega, with a top speed of 195 mph, was outclassed by competing state of the art air racers which reached more than 300 mph. The race was a rough one as one competitor, Cecil Allen, died in a fiery takeoff crash, and rival Jacqueline Cochran was forced to withdraw due to mechanical problems, the fog, and violent thunderstorms that plagued the race.

Left, Amelia Earhart giving the 1935 Amelia Earhart Trophy to winner, 22 year old Melba Beard in Cleveland, OH. Right, an image of the Bendix Trophy, competition for which was banned for women pilots for some years.

30

MID-WEEK PICTORIAL

"NEWS OF THE WORLD IN PICTURES"

VOL. XL, NO. 23   PRICE TEN CENTS

NEW YORK, WEEK ENDING JANUARY 19, 1935

FIRST TO FLY SOLO FROM HAWAII TO CALIFORNIA
Amelia Earhart, Who Was the First Woman to Fly Alone Across the Atlantic, Receiving Congratulations at
Oakland, Calif., After Flying the 2,400 Miles From Honolulu in 18 Hours and 16 Minutes.
(Times Wide World Photos, San Francisco Bureau.)

January 19, 1935 Mid-Week Pictorial heralding Earhart's
record-setting flight from Honolulu to Oakland. (from
author's collection)

31

Amelia Earhart flanked by two guests, unidentified

Hand tinted by Chris Taylore, Atchison County Hist. Society

Left, a sketch of Earhart from the Atchison newspaper ca 1935; Above, a close-up of Earhart on her float during the parade on June 7, 1935.

Amelia Earhart addressing Atchison in Memorial Hall on June 7, 1935

Earhart in one of her most familiar roles—that of spokesperson for
commercial aviation, in this case, American Airways, later American
Airlines, 1935. (Courtesy American Airlines)

Colorization by David K. Bowman

Above, l to r, GP Putnam, Amelia Earhart and Paul Mantz; Above right, Earhart and GP Putnam, at the 1935 Cleveland Air Races; Below, left, a picture of Earhart and three unidentified men at the Lockheed plant in Burbank, CA in approximately 1932; right, a 1935 magazine ad in which Earhart endorsed safety precautions for ocean fliers.

Above left, Earhart in class at Purdue; above right, a statue outside the
present day Amelia Earhart Residence Hall at Purdue

In mid 1935 Earhart joined the faculty of Purdue University in as a visiting faculty member to counsel women on careers and as a technical advisor to the Department of Aeronautics. Not long afterward, Earhart began planning a round-the-world flight. It was not the first flight to circle the globe, but it would be the longest at 29,000 miles following an equatorial route. Purdue set up a special fund to purchase a plane for Earhart from donations, eventually raising about $80,000, which would around $1 million in current money with an adjustment for inflation. Earhart settled on a twin-engined Lockheed Model 10E, which she later dubbed her "Flying Laboratory. The source of the funding remains controversial. The Electra was built at Lockheed Aircraft Company to her specifications which included extensive modifications to the fuselage to incorporate a large fuel tank. Earhart took delivery of her new airship on July 24, 1936, her birthday and placed the craft in a hangar at Paul Mantz's United Air Services, which was located just across the airfield from Lockheed's Burbank plant, where the plane had been built.

1963 U.S. airmail stamp
in Earhart's honor with
iconic pose

Earhart in front of her new airship on July 24, 1936, her birthday

Colorization by David K. Bowman

35

Chapter 9

Final Flight

Although the Electra was publicized as a "flying laboratory," no immediate scientific activity was planned, with the plane initially dedicated to the round-the-world flight, during which Earhart would gather material for her next book. Her first choice as navigator was Captain Harry Manning, who had been the captain of the President Roosevelt, the ship that had brought Earhart back from Europe in 1928.

Earhart and her principal navigator, Captain Harry Manning, February 1937

Amelia Earhart studying charts in early 1937.

However, through contacts in the Los Angeles aviation community, Frederick Noonan, a renowned navigator for Pan American Airways, was subsequently chosen as a back-up navigator. This was because although Manning was a superb nautical navigator, Earhart recognized the need to have a competent aerial navigator on the flight. Noonan had vast experience in both aerial and marine navigation, as he was a licensed ship's captain and flight navigator, as well. Noonan had recently left Pan American, where he had blazed trails, establishing most of the company's China Clipper seaplane routes across the Pacific. Noonan had also been responsible for training Pan America's navigators for the route between San Francisco and Manila. He had unfortunately been terminated by Pan American for a drinking problem, which caused some consternation on Earhart's part, although Earhart agreed to hire Noonan as act-up navigator on the advice of Paul Mantz and her husband. The original plan was for Noonan to navigate from Hawaii to Howland Island, a particularly difficult portion of the flight, then Manning would continue with Earhart to Australia and she would proceed on her own for the remainder of the flight.

Who was Frederick Noonan?

Fred Noonan, ca
early 1930s

Frederick J. Noonan was a figure more enigmatic than Amelia Earhart. Oddly, his birth certificate is reportedly not on file, and Noonan was also an eerie lookalike for aviation colleague William VanDusen, which confused coworkers at Pan American and later provided some confusion for researchers. Moreover, Noonan was reported to be a naval reserve officer with some connection to intelligence. An exceptionally intelligent man, Noonan was, by the mid 1930s, one of the only, and also one of the greatest aerial navigators on earth, which is what caught the interest of G.P. Putnam and Paul Mantz. Noonan is reported to have almost invented the field during the time he mapped aerial routes over the Pacific for Pan American Airlines.

Noonan was born in Chicago, Illinois on April 4, 1893 to Joseph T. Noonan and Catherine Egan who was English. His father died when Noonan was four, and in the summer of 1905 Noonan went to Seattle, Washington, eventually finding work as a seaman.

When he was seventeen, Noonan shipped out of Seattle as an ordinary seaman on a British sailing bark, the *Crompton*. Between 1910 and 1915, he worked on over a dozen ships, rising to the ratings of quartermaster and bosun's mate. He continued working on merchant marine ships throughout WWI, serving as an officer on ammunition ships. His wartime service included the terrifying experience of having three different vessels torpedoed from under him by German U-Boats. After the war, Noonan continued to work in the Merchant Marine, achieving a good reputation as a ship's officer. Noonan's maritime career during the 1920s flourished, as his ratings increased to usually the highest marks in his work performance reviews. In 1927, Noonan married Josephine Sullivan at Jackson, Mississippi. The two remained married until the spring of 1937, when Noonan divorced his wife to marry Beatrice Martinelli.

By the late 1920s Noonan had decided on a career change, and received a limited commercial pilot's license in 1930. That same year, he had also gone to work for Pan American and was made airport manager at Port Au Prince, Haiti. Later, Noonan was made inspector of all of Pan American's airports. In 1931, Noonan was granted master's papers, which qualified him to be the captain of a merchant marine ship. During the early to mid 1930s, Noonan was chief navigator for Pan American and mapped all the aerial routes in the Pacific Ocean for the famed Pan American Clipper flights.

Left, William Van Dusen Ca. appx. 1975; both Noonan and Van Dusen shared a remarkable resemblance and both men's birth records were elusive; Right, Fred Noonan and Amelia Earhart ca 1937

Above, candid photo of
Frederick Noonan ca 1937

By December 1936, when Noonan met Amelia Earhart, he was reported by some sources to have been discharged by Pan American for heavy drinking, and by other sources to have resigned his job because he felt he had gone as far as he could with Pan American. He was a man at the crossroads of his life and a flight with Amelia Earhart represented pretty much his last chance in aerial navigation. Initially, Noonan's reputation for drinking disturbed and alarmed Earhart, who did not want to take Noonan on as a navigator. It was at the urging of her husband G.P. Putnam and technical advisor Paul Mantz that Earhart reluctantly agreed to take on Noonan as back-up navigator. Both Putnam and Mantz felt that Noonan's much vaunted expertise in aerial navigation was important for the flight, as Harry Manning, who had already been designated principal navigator, was only qualified in nautical navigation. After Earhart's crash at Luke Field in March 1937, Manning backed out of the flight, leaving Noonan as principal navigator. Oddly, by then, positions were reversed. G.P. and Mantz both wanted Noonan to be let go, and Earhart wanted to keep Noonan. Earhart prevailed. She was not gong to be the one to foreclose Fred Noonan's last chance at a career in navigation.

Courtesy of nickgrantadventures.com

Above, a program for the inaugural flight of the China Clipper, November 22, 1935; note Fred Noonan, third from left; l., a reproduction of an old postcard showing one of the legendary Pan American China Clippers over equally legendary San Francisco in the mid 1930s.

Left to right, clockwise: Upper left corner, Earhart and Paul Mantz on a test flight; above, Earhart and Mantz conferring; Below, Earhart in an iconic photo taken September 1936; Lower right, casual shot of Earhart 1936-7; Lower left corner, Earhart with her plane, February 1937; and center left, GP and Earhart planning in their study.

Colorization by David K. Bowman

colorization by David K. Bowman

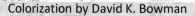

Colorization by David K. Bowman

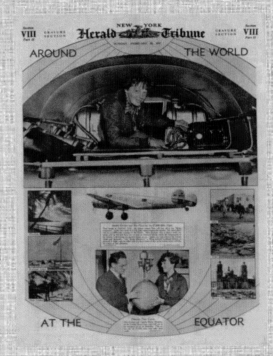

Colorization by David K. Bowman

Above, left, February 1937 New York Herald Tribune section devoted to the last flight; above right, a great photo of Earhart by Albert Breslin, her personal photographer

On March 17, 1937, St. Patrick's Day, Earhart and her crew flew the first leg of their round the world flight from Oakland, California to Honolulu, Hawaii. I addition to Earhart and Noonan, Harry Manning and Paul Mantz, who was acting as Earhart's technical advisor were onboard. When they reached Honolulu, it was discovered there were problems with the lubrication of the propellers. Due to the lack of time and facilities, Mantz wasn't able to have them completely serviced. After all the work possible was done on the propellers, the flight was scheduled for Luke Field, in Pearl Harbor.

Below left, l to r: Paul Mantz; Amelia Earhart; Elmer Dimity, manager; and Nellie G. Donohoe, Oakland Postmaster; and, below right, a group shot of Paul Mantz, Amelia Earhart, Harry Manning, and Fred Noonan in Oakland, CA. Both photos taken on March 17, 1937

Early on the morning of March 20, 1937, with Noonan and Manning on board, Earhart ran into trouble. Her craft went into a ground loop and finally came to a crashing halt. The Electra would require massive work to make it airworthy again. The circumstances of the ground loop are still not clearly explained and remain controversial. Some witnesses at Luke Field, including the Associated Press journalists on scene said they saw a tire blow. Earhart thought either the Electra's right tire had blown out/or the right landing gear had collapsed. Several others, including Paul Mantz thought it was pilot error.

Left, just after the crash; Below, a while later, after daylight

The flight was called off and the aircraft was shipped by sea to the Lockheed facility in Burbank, California for repairs. At this point, Harry Manning left the flight and Fred Noonan agreed to be the principal navigator. Concerns over his reliability increased.

41

While the Electra was being repaired, Earhart and her husband worked to secure additional funds and prepared for a second attempt. The new flight plan, however, called for a flight from west to east, and quietly began with an unpublicized departure from Oakland on May 21, 1937. She stopped at a couple of places along the way, arriving in Miami on May 23, 1937. The idea was that if anything went wrong, they could turn back without any undue publicity. In Miami, Earhart publicly announced her plans to circumnavigate the globe. The flight's opposite direction was explained as the result of changes in global wind and weather patterns along the planned route since the earlier attempt. Fred Noonan would now be aboard the entire flight. They departed Miami on June 1 and after numerous stops in South America, Africa, the Indian subcontinent and Southeast Asia, arrived at Lae, New Guinea on June 29, 1937. At this stage, about 22,000 miles of the journey had been completed with 7,000 remaining, almost all over the Pacific.

Second Round the World Attempt
May 21, 1937

Left, Amelia Earhart and Fred Noonan in Los Angeles the night before their takeoff from Oakland in May 1937; Above Amelia Earhart Putnam being welcomed in Caripito, Venezuela by, third from right, Andres Roland, governor of the state of Mongas; Henry E Linam, Standard Oil executive, fourth from right. The others are unidentified. Lower left, a beautiful view from the air of Puerto Rico; Below, Amelia Earhart and Fred Noonan entering their plane in Puerto Rico.

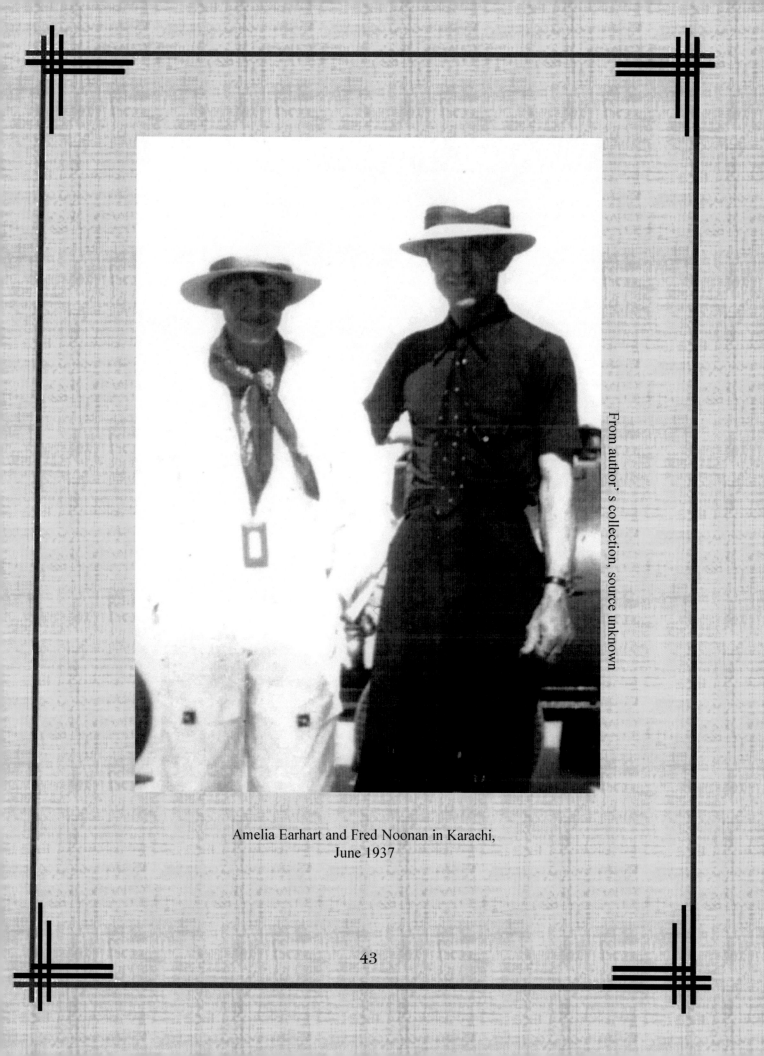

From author's collection, source unknown

Amelia Earhart and Fred Noonan in Karachi,
June 1937

From l to r, clockwise: Above, Fortaleza; Natal; Karachi, Sudan; and Dakar

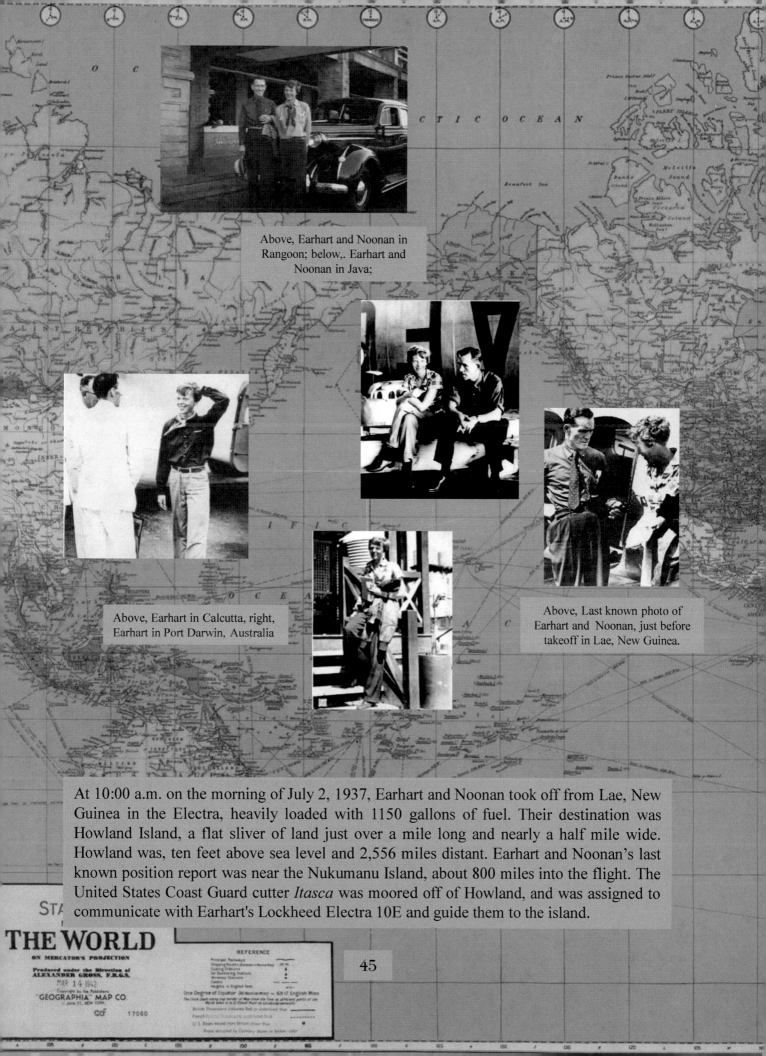

Above, Earhart and Noonan in Rangoon; below,. Earhart and Noonan in Java;

Above, Earhart in Calcutta, right, Earhart in Port Darwin, Australia

Above, Last known photo of Earhart and Noonan, just before takeoff in Lae, New Guinea.

At 10:00 a.m. on the morning of July 2, 1937, Earhart and Noonan took off from Lae, New Guinea in the Electra, heavily loaded with 1150 gallons of fuel. Their destination was Howland Island, a flat sliver of land just over a mile long and nearly a half mile wide. Howland was, ten feet above sea level and 2,556 miles distant. Earhart and Noonan's last known position report was near the Nukumanu Island, about 800 miles into the flight. The United States Coast Guard cutter *Itasca* was moored off of Howland, and was assigned to communicate with Earhart's Lockheed Electra 10E and guide them to the island.

THE WORLD
ON MERCATOR'S PROJECTION
Produced under the Direction of
ALEXANDER GROSS, F.R.G.S.
MAR 14 1942
Copyright by the Publishers
"GEOGRAPHIA" MAP CO.
JOHN ST. NEW YORK.

ccf   17060

REFERENCE

Chapter 11

The Unthinkable – KHAQQ Calling ITASCA., SOS!

L to r, clockwise, Amelia Earhart .taking off from Lae, New Guinea on 2 July 1937; last known photo of Fred Noonan and Amelia Earhart at Lae, New Guinea; the cutter ITASCA; Chief Radioman Leo Bellarts; and a 1937 chart of Howland Island.

Something went seriously wrong during the flight, which climaxed with the Electra disappearing at an unknown location. The government and media reported that Earhart had ditched not far from the *Itasca*, due to her radio signal strength, which was an S5 (the strongest signal strength). But to this day, multiple attempts to search the sea near Howland Island have been unsuccessful. In 2010, the Waite Institute, upon completion of their search, declared that as far as they were concerned, Earhart's plane was not in the sea near Howland.

First three: Radio logs of USCGC ITASCA; last image: HOWLAND ISLAND log (RM2 Cipriani)

AMELIA FEARED LOST!

$100,000 Bond Issue for S. M. Schools Proposed

Mrs. Cooke To Get Notice But Will Lose Job

Harry French Found Guilty In Feud Killing

S. F. GRAND JURY TO ASK THAT POLICE BOARD QUIT

Rapheld and Maybe Chief Quinn To Be Included

NAVY SHIPS ORDERED TO BEGIN HUNT

Plane Over 2500-Mile Pacific Waste

ISLAND IS GOAL

Newspaper front page appearing a few days after Earhart disappeared

47

'They Failed to Arrive,'—And Another Tragedy Marks Air Progress

Miss Earhart Was Aviation 'Realist'

The glamor of her flying achievements has been such that few persons know Amelia Earhart Putnam is ranking in her own right, a linguist and a brilliant student with outstanding research work in experimental and calculative contributory to her credit.

A tall, slim woman with a shock of curly hair she sometimes is described as the feminine counterpart of Lindbergh—she looks decidedly like national prominence in June, 1928, as only a passenger on the transatlantic flight of Wilmer Stultz and Louis Gordon.

At that time she was an obscure social worker in Boston and only two or three of her friends knew she had been flying since she was and had held the 17th international license ever issued. But her zest caught the popular imagination and when the flight from Newfoundland ended at Wales after 20 hours and 49 minutes she was held up as the "heroine."

A Realist

Always a realist Mrs. Putnam belittled her own part in the undertaking, but vowed to her friends that some day she would fly the Atlantic by herself. From then on she occupied herself too with her aeronautical work—giving extension courses in English to New England factory workers—and went into training for the flights.

Her background for a feat of this magnitude was more than adequate. Born in Atchison, Kan., July 24, 1898, she became interested in flying in her teens. Her father, Edwin S. Earhart, an attorney, opposed her interest because it was too dangerous but he admitted there was nothing to prevent her buying "two or three planes if she wanted them."

At 17 she did war work in Toronto and after she was resumed she got into nursing studies which had taken her through Ogontz school at Jenkintown, Pa., with advanced work at Harvard, Columbia and the University of California. She learned five languages fluently. While in California she started her aviation lessons.

Early Woman Flier

She was one of the earliest women fliers, making her first solo flight in 1921 after only 10 hours of instruction. Within two years she set a woman's altitude mark of 14,000 feet and a year later received the coveted license of the Federation Aeronautique Internationale—the first woman so designated.

After the flight with Stultz and Gordon the flier courted writing a book about the feat and formed the friend of the publisher. George Palmer Putnam and to wife later Mrs. Putnam divorced her husband and Mrs. Earhart and Putnam were married Feb. 7, 1931.

While Putnam was too conservative himself to offer inspiration she too was flying. In 1935 Mrs. Putnam flew to Hawaii to be the first person to make a solo flight from the islands to the mainland. She landed 18 hours and 16 minutes later near Landonferry, Ireland, the fastest transatlantic flight on record.

Wanted by Balchen

Bernt Balchen, famed aviator, wanted Mrs. Putnam to bear the take-off and to attempt the flight that, day because of her competence which came too to have out the wings. But hours were just ...

Next she set a non-stop record when she flew from Mexico to New York.

Active Year

For the rest of that year and the following year of 1936 Amelia Earhart devoted her energies to including on aviation. But before the year was over, she was growing restless to fly again. Then time she wanted to attempt the greatest task in her career. She announced briefly that she was going to try an round-the-world flight.

On March 17, 1937, Mrs Earhart took off from Oakland, Cal. for Honolulu, accompanied by Paul Mantz, her technical adviser; Fred J. Noonan, co-navigator and Capt. Harry Manning, navigator. Amelia succeeded in making the 2,410 mile trip in the record time of 15 hours 47 minutes. But the takeoff near...

The round-the-world flight was temporarily halted. When she took off for Howland island, Miss Earhart's plane skidded, blew out a tire and cracked. But the woman flier was not daunted.

Two months later, she was ready to try again. This time, her route was charted from west to east. She and Fred Noonan flew from Burbank, Cal., to Miami, Fla., the starting point.

On June 1, 1937, Miss Earhart and her navigator took off from Miami.

Their first stop was Puerto Rico. From then on, they flew in short flights in Natal, Brazil, and from Natal, the flying couple spanned the South Atlantic and arrived at St. Louis, Senegal, on June ...

They conquered their next hazard—Africa—in six days, landing at Assab, Eritrea, on the Red Sea on June 14. Karachi, India, was their next stop—a flight of 1,390 miles. From Karachi, Amelia Earhart and her navigator flew on to Calcutta three days later. Next, they reached Port Darwin, Australia, flying over Rangoon, Singapore, Bandoeng, Sourabaya and Kupang. On June 28, they reached Lae, New Guinea, after a 1,200 mile flight from Port Darwin. Their next scheduled stop was Howland Island, Oceania, a 2,580 mile trip. They expected to cover this in 18 hours. They left Lae at 8 p. m. CST July 1. They failed to arrive at this island, a sea and a half mile spit of sand.

Feminine Lindbergh

MRS. AMELIA EARHART PUTNAM

Pacific Question Mark

... a two and a half mile spit of sand.

'A Scientist'—

... outstanding research work ...

Next Stop?

EARHART   NOONAN

Trans-Atlantic Record

'Great Ovation'

... 14 hours and 56 minutes later ... a record ...

Her Rewards

... set a record ...

But Manning Stayed Behind---This Time

Captain Harry Manning was her navigator on a previous flight. But on the flight that has ended somewhere in the vast wastes of the Pacific, Fred Noonan accompanied her in the "Flying Laboratory."

Genealogical Department
Directed by Mrs. Norman T. Gill

(column of genealogical text, largely illegible)

28 Madison Men to Attend Saengerfest

(column text, largely illegible)

Rierson Awarded Badger Contract

(column text, largely illegible)

Duffy to Back Barkley, Court Bill

By RUBY A. BLACK
(State Journal Washington Bureau)
WASHINGTON — Sen. F. Ryan Duffy of Wisconsin took this week by Sen. F. Ryan Duffy, Fond du Lac democrat, his decide clearly his support of the compromise judiciary reorganization bill. They are ...

Land Commission Approves Loans

(column text, largely illegible)

East Side News

(column text, largely illegible)

Optometrists Meet Here Monday

(column text, largely illegible)

Newspaper front page appearing after Earhart had been given up for dead

Above left, an issue from a series in which G.P. Putnam serialized SOARING WINGS in the winter and spring of 1939; above right an issue of Pacific Islands Monthly from May 1938, with an article about a letter to Earhart in the Jaluit post office; below left cover of the September 10, 1944 issue of AMERICAN WEEKLY and , right, the article in it about Earhart's disappearance.

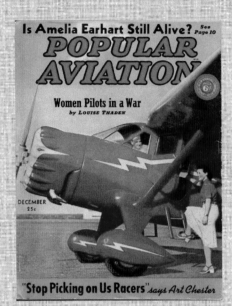

Upper two magazine covers are for December 1939/January 1940 issues containing the story IS AMELA EARHART STILL ALIVE?; Below, the January 1940 issue of TRUE DETECTIVE, containing the story TRAPPING THE AMELIA EARHART EXTORTION GHOULS, about Wilbur Rothar.

The Cleveland Plain Dealer

Wonderful art deco graphics highlight this informative 1982 article. Above, the issue cover and right, the first two pages of the article. The article contains a revealing interview Earhart's secretary Margot DeCarie and describes the investigation into Earhart's disappearance by the Kotheras. Impressive art deco graphics!

Smith's Weekly

FOUNDED BY JOYNTON SMITH — The Public Guardian
Vol. XIX, No. 38 (Copyright)   Saturday, October 16, 1937
PRICE 4d

"SMITH'S" VAUDEVILLIANS—NOT WASTING ANY WORDS

U.S.A. does AUSTRALIA a Secret Service

AMELIA EARHART SEARCH MADE THE OPPORTUNITY

Plane Observers Over Japanese Pacific Bases

TIP WAS GIVEN OUR DEFENCE DEPT.

WHEN W. M. Hughes, at the Peace Conference, insisted that Japan have no island mandates in the Pacific below the Equator, he was longsighted.

But even with what Japan has, her strategists have not been idle. Australian defence authorities know all about this now. U.S.A. observers seized the opportunity offered by the search for Amelia Earhart. They swept wide enough to make a scrutiny of Japanese naval activities in islands in the groups under control of Nippon.

UNTIL now the real story has been withheld of the desperate international intrigue, blanketing Australia, that went with the search for ill-fated Amelia Earhart, when that intrepid aviatrix crashed into the Pacific somewhere near the Phoenix Islands.

IT is a story of military tactics that would have to hand with the deep secret—hand with the terrific success of $200,000 spent by American naval planes.

OUR PACIFIC NEIGHBORS—Or should it be Our Neighbors in the Pacific?

AUSTRALIA Would Have NO PETROL In Event Of WAR

Only Three Months' Stock Kept In Reserve

IF, by some calamity, Australia were isolated from the rest of the world tomorrow, she would have only three months' supplies of petrol. When that had been consumed, EVERY AEROPLANE AND AUTOMOBILE IN THE COUNTRY WOULD BE USELESS.

AUSTRALIA is one of the most highly mechanised countries in the world, and the eighth largest consumer of petrol, according to world statistics for 1936.

Grim News For War Department

FIRST IMPRESSIONS

PRIME Minister's babybonus song: "Just before the battle, mother, I was thinking most of you."

NESTLÉ'S PURE THICK CREAM

Last part of the article in the October 13, 1937
Smith's Weekly

Courtesy www.chilhour.com

Courtesy of www.flic.kr.com

Courtesy of Evs-islands.com

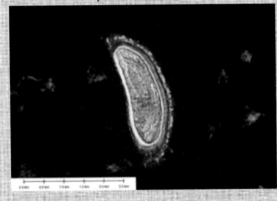

Above left, aerial photo of Howland Island; above, the beach at Howland Island; left, satellite photo of Howland Island; below, left, a forlorn view of the Amelia Earhart Beacon from a nearby sign; below right, a close up shot of the Amelia Earhart Beacon standing its lonely vigil.

Courtesy of www.tripsmithy.com

Courtesy of www.unc.edu

54

Theories Regarding the Disappearance of Amelia Earhart

The following represents all the significant theories that have emerged in published materials. There are other theories which are variations on them, and were not included, as it served no purpose. As well, there are a number of "fringe" theories that were not included, due to the lack of any substance.

As of this date, no theory has been conclusively proven.

"CRASHED AND SUNK"

This theory, now questioned by many, was the original explanation of Earhart's disappearance reported by the government in the media. It holds that she ran out of gas and crashed into the sea within approximately 40 miles of Howland Island. Proponents of the theory maintain that Earhart encountered heavy headwinds during her flight to Howland Island and ran low on fuel. Nearing Howland Island, according to proponents, Earhart suddenly ran out of fuel and crashed into the sea, her aircraft sinking immediately.

Other supporters included Paul Mantz, Ron Bright, and RMC Leo Bellarts. Rearchers Elgen and Marie Long, as wells as Walter Roessler and Leo Gomez haze supported this theory in their books despite the extensive new information regarding Earhart's disappearance that has been developed since 1937.

Supporting evidence for theory:

The main arguments in support of the theory are that a high signal strength, S-5, was reported by the ITASCA just before radio contact was lost with Earhart. Also, heavy weather had been reported west of Howland Island before Earhart disappeared, which some researchers feel caused her to exhaust her supply of fuel prematurely.

Factors mitigating against the theory are:

☐ No hard evidence has ever been found that Earhart crashed into the sea near Howland Island.
☐ Credible radio messages were picked up from Earhart for up to ten days after her disappearance. Credible evidence from other sources places Earhart's Electra on the island of Saipan in 1944.
☐ Credible evidence from other sources indicates Earhart came down elsewhere, probably in the Marshall Islands.

 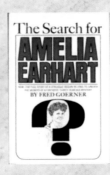 

"CRASHED, PICKED UP AND LATER DIED"

This is a widely held belief, and not improbable, as Saipan was the administrative headquarters of the Japanese military in the Pacific. Adherents feel that she ran out of gas, or was forced down, probably in the Marshall Islands near Mili Atoll, and was later taken to Saipan. There, she died or was executed by the Japanese.

The theory originated in 1944 following a U.S. military investigation after the retaking of the Central Pacific. There were later investigations by Paul Briand, Fred Goerner, Thomas Devine, and Mike Campbell. Other noted supporters include Buddy Brennan and Don Wilson.

Thomas Devine reported receiving verbal confirmation of the guard at a hanger at Aslito Field that the hangar contained the airplane of Amelia Earhart. Devine also reported that he saw Amelia Earhart's plane on a number of occasions, most on the same day. He reported noting Earhart's CAA number, NR16020, on the aircraft. He saw the aircraft:

- First in the afternoon, taking off from Aslito Field for a short flight
- Later, in the early evening, parked on the tarmac at Aslito Field, where he viewed the aircraft up close, looked in the cockpit, and touched it
- Still later the same evening, after the aircraft had been set on fire by American forces
- As a burned out shell near Aslito Field, during the rest of his year on Saipan

Devine also claimed to have been shown Amelia Earhart's gravesite by a local woman in 1945. He was never able to excavate the site.

The supporting evidence for theory include highly credible eyewitness testimony of Thomas Devine and other servicemen stationed on Saipan, significant eyewitness evidence indicating Earhart came down in the area of the Marshall Islands and highly credible evidence indicating that the Office of Naval Intelligence placed Devine under surveillance during his 1961 trip to the home of Muriel Earhart Morrissey

On the other hand, Devine was never able to excavate the gravesite he was shown and thus produce hard evidence that Earhart perished on Saipan.

"CRASHED, PICKED UP, SURVIVED AND REPATRIATED"

This theory was originally speculated about not long after Earhart's disappearance and held by Earhart's mother. It held that she ran out of gas, or was forced down, probably in the Marshall Islands near Mili Atoll and then was later taken to Saipan, Japan or China, and survived her captivity and was repatriated to the USA at the end of WW II. According to one variation, she was later secretly repatriated by Msgr. James Kelley, on the order of the Pope and with the assistance of the U.S. Government.

New impetus was given the theory by AMELIA EARHART LIVES, published in 1970 by Joseph Gervais and Joseph Klaas. Noted supporters are Tod Swindell, Rollin Reineck, and Irene Bolam's sister in law, Irene Bolam Plymate.

The supporting evidence for theory includes

❑ Credible photo study commissioned by Tod Swindell, with some images of a woman calling herself Irene Bolam which demonstrate exact coincidence with the bone structure of Amelia Earhart both facially and in her hands.

❑ The strong feeling of many friends of a woman calling herself Irene Bolam, including her own personal physician, that she was in fact Amelia Earhart. These feelings were based on the woman's startling physical resemblance to Amelia Earhart, plus numerous instances of odd behavior and statements of the woman.

❑ Discoveries, during Tod Swindell's photo study, of a *second* Irene Bolam. The discovery was made in an analysis of most of the photos of a woman, purporting to be Irene Bolam, printed in a series of 1982 New Jersey newspaper articles on Amelia Earhart. Analysis showed she was neither the real Irene Bolam nor Amelia Earhart. These photos seemed an attempt by someone to discredit the Bolam theory with the public.

Factors discrediting the theory include:

❑ Lack of any plausible explanation of why Amelia Earhart would have wanted to abandon her life and friends. Msgr. Kelley, whose statements were quoted by the theory supporters as a confirmation of their concept was later shown to have been suffering from mental deterioration in his final years, leaving his assertions at question.
❑ The forensic study of 2002 has yet to be formally finalized.
❑ Some people from Irene Bolam's earlier life disputed the theory, and there is controversy over the height of Irene Bolam.

"FORCED DOWN NEAR HULL ISLAND, DIED IN AMERICAN SAMOA"

This theory holds that she reached Howland Island, did not land, continued on to the area of Hull Island, and ditched on the shore. Later, she was picked up by Capt. Jones, RNR, who was stationed on Hull Island, and eventually taken to American Samoa. There, on Aunu'u Island, in protective custody, Earhart perished of dysentery and Noonan drowned in the surf while trying to escape the island. This theory was advanced by researcher James Donahue and is not heavily supported, although it is intriguing. Mr. Donohue's book is relatively rare, frequently expensive but profusely illustrated with photos and charts.

The evidence supporting the theory is threefold:

☐ Radio signals triangulated by Pan American Airways as coming from the area of Hull Island

☐ Ships' logs in various archives in the Pacific area, (Fiji, New Zealand, Australia, etc.)

☐ The Morgenthau telephone transcript

The main factor discrediting the theory is a lack of evidence. Donahue repeatedly cited "archival" evidence as proof, but did not clearly outline or identify of this evidence in his book

"FORCED DOWN NEAR SIDNEY ISLAND, CAPTURED, SURVIVED"

This theory surfaced with the 1985 publication of STAND BY TO DIE by Robert Myers. Myers claimed to have befriended Earhart during visits to the Oakland Airport and been told by her before she left on her last flight that she was on a mission for the government. Myers reported seeing Earhart's plane fitted with Ping-Pong balls for increased buoyancy. He also claimed to have listened, after Earhart's loss, to Earhart's and ITASCA's broadcasts for 8-10 days on the family radio. He maintained that Earhart's broadcasts detailed her entire flight from Lae until her ditching. Myers maintained that she was bracketed by Japanese fighters, which forced her down in the area of Sidney Island. Eight to ten days later, she was picked up by the Japanese and held in captivity until the end of WW II.

He also claimed to have met personally with Earhart, who was living under the name of Irene Bolam, a short while before her death in 1982.

Supporting evidence for theory is that

☐ There are indications from various sources that Earhart was flying a mission for the government

☐ Myers located a man named Rollo Christy who he said corroborated his observations of Ping-Pong balls aboard Earhart's Electra.

Factors discrediting theory are the foillowing:

☐ There is credible evidence from other sources that Earhart was picked up by the Japanese elsewhere
☐ There are no accounts corroborating the content of the radio transmissions Robert Myers reported.
☐ Those who interviewed Myers after publication of his book in 1985 reported signs of marked mental instability, thus leaving Myers' assertions at question.

"NEW BRITAIN"

This theory originated with Australian military personnel who were serving on the island of New Britain during WW II. The theory was later investigated by research David Billings. It holds that through navigational error, Earhart flew back in the direction from which she came. She finally crashed on the Island of New Britain, perishing, along with Noonan, in the process.

In 1945, an Australian Army patrol found the wreckage of what appeared to be a twin engine airplane on the island of New Britain. Upon inspecting the wreck, they found an engine with a metal tag on it engraved with, among other things: S3HI C/N 1055. This was found to be significant years later because Amelia Earhart's Electra was equipped with Pratt & Whitney R-1340-S3H1 engines. In addition, the Lockheed serial number was 1055.

Supporting evidence for theory is the patrol map with markings on it from the aircraft engine tag. Mitigating against th theory is the fact that Earhart would not have had enough fuel to have flown to the area of Howland Island then have flown back to New Britain, which is not far from Lae, New Guinea. Billings has not yet satisfactorily explained this problem.

"TINIAN"

This theory originated from St. John Naftel, who served on Tinian during WWII. Naftel claimed a laborer on the island showed him the place where Earhart and Noonan had been buried b y the Japanese. His theory was that she ditched somewhere in the Central Pacific and was taken to Saipan. After a time, she and Noonan were executed. They were then taken to the neighboring island of Tinian and buried there.

Supporting evidence for theory is 1) Strong evidence from other sources that Earhart was held prisoner on Saipan; 2) The account of the worker on Tinian during WWII, and 3) That Naftel was shown a site he believed to be a gravesite.

The main factor discrediting theory is that excavations on Tinian in late 2004 failed to disclose any evidence Earhart had been buried there. Researcher Jerry Wilson investigated the theory.

"NIKUMARORO ISLAND"

This theory originated with Richard Gillespie, director of TIGHAR (The International Group for Historic Aircraft Recovery). The theory holds that through navigational error, Earhart overshot Howland Island and continued southeast to Nikumaroro Island, which was then called Gardner Island. She ditched on the north shore of the island and broadcast SOS messages for some days. Finally, the Electra was washed off the shore into deep water by a storm and Earhart and Noonan, unable to have salvaged enough of their supplies, perished from heat, thirst and starvation.

TIGHAR has mounted multiple expeditions to Nikumaroro, which have uncovered:

- ☐ A 1930s vintage, size 9 shoe sole, owner unknown
- ☐ A piece of sheet metal from an unknown type of aircraft
- ☐ A metal navigator's bookcase from an unknown type of aircraft

The main supporting evidence for theory is 1) Earhart's last reported position and direction of flight (she was flying on a line of position in either a northwesterly or southeasterly direction), and 2) A number of the "post loss" radio messages suggest that Earhart had landed on land. Factors discrediting theory are that 1) No connection has been established between Amelia Earhart and the artifacts recovered from Nikumaroro; and 2) No other evidence has been found on Nikumaroro that Earhart may have ditched there; and 3) Significant evidence indicates Earhart ditched elsewhere and places her, Fred Noonan, and her plane on Saipan after her disappearance.

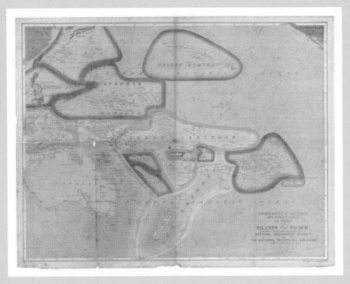

1921 map showing the various League of Nations
Mandates in the Central Pacific area

Islands of Mystery
The State of Affairs in the Pacific in 1937

A central factor in the disappearance of Amelia Earhart was the political situation at the time of her round-the-world flight. At the time, Franklin Roosevelt, or "FDR" as he was known, was in the oval office. The world of the mid 1930s was filled with tension, suspicion, aggression, war.

Having served as Assistant Secretary of the Navy for the Office of Naval Intelligence during WWI, FDR came to the presidency with unprecedented experience in and fascination with intelligence. Coupled with his fascination with intelligence, he had a great propensity for secrecy, which has only become apparent in recent decades. For him, intelligence blended with politics into a subtle and ruthless game, which he played with consummate skill.

Many of Roosevelt's secret activities turned out to be well taken and well advised, but some of them were less forthcoming in intent, having the flavor of almost a secret international chess game. Much may never be known of these, as he never put a lot of things in writing. This was in marked contrast to the policy of later presidents such as Kennedy, Johnson, and Nixon, who tried to tape record every word uttered in the oval office.

One of FDR's typical procedures was to route his outgoing message traffic through U.S. Army communications, and incoming messages through U.S. Navy facilities. As a result, only the files in his "Map Room" were complete, and nobody in either armed service had a complete overview of his message activity.

Until 1941, when the Office of Information Coordination (OIC) was established, intelligence collection methods of the government were not always very organized. The OIC would become the Office of Strategic Services (OSS), which would eventually become the Central Intelligence Agency (CIA) in 1947.

During the 1930s, FDR was noted for asking wealthy and well-connected friends and amateurs to accept intelligence assignments during their travels. Although FDR had at his disposal excellent signal intelligence (intercepted radio messages, etc.), he placed a far greater confidence in intelligence gathered through human means by spies.

The epitome of his fixation on human intelligence was a group called "The Room." It was an intelligence gathering group of wealthy, highly-placed people in FDR's circle, which was organized and run by publisher Vincent Astor. FDR's dream was of establishing a vast elaborate network of intelligence operatives to penetrate any government or any facility.

Astor had created "The Room" in 1927 as a purely recreational exercise in low level intelligence gathering with a number of wealthy friends. Astor's fellow members included, among others, Theodore Roosevelt's brother Kermit; banker Winthrop W. Aldrich; diplomat David E. Bruce; publisher Nelson Doubleday and philanthropist Rhinelander Stewart.

The group met monthly in an innocuous apartment at 34 East 62nd Street in New York City, which was equipped with a mail drop and an unlisted phone. A close and select group, they swapped gossip and low-grade intelligence. Occasionally entertaining, they invited persons such as Somerset Maugham and Commander Richard E. Byrd to speak.

After Roosevelt ascended to the presidency, Astor's quiet informal network of globe-trotting wealthy friends became an important and regular intelligence source for FDR. In the tense world of the 1930s, the government needed all the intelligence it could get to deal with an impending war. Seen in that light, it would be almost inconceivable that an around the world flight proposed by an internationally famous and beloved aviatrix would fail to be seen as the ideal vehicle for some sort of intelligence gathering.

As FDR played things according to a crisp set of rules, including "if you're caught, you're on your own", Earhart's flight would be an eerie precursor of the U-2 affair of 1960. That incident involved military pilot Gary Francis Powers, who flew U-2 surveillance planes for the CIA. Shot down in 1960, he was taken prisoner, and endured a harrowing period of captivity before the Russians finally released him. Initially, the U.S. Government disowned Powers' surveillance flight. It was only massive publicity, which forced the issue into the open.

In the world at large in the 1930s, there was deep trouble in all directions. In Europe, Adolf Hitler and his National Socialist Party were on the rise. In 1933, the National Socialist Party gained control of the Reichstag, electing Hitler as the head of the government. Almost immediately, Hitler initiated his grisly holocaust and made plans to begin annexing Europe. In 1935, Italy invaded Ethiopia, which provoked deep concern on the part of the various western allies, who began to fear additional Italian aggression would occur at any time along the Mediterranean.

In the Pacific Area, things were also becoming serious. In 1919, after WWI, Japan had been mandated the Caroline, Marshall, and Marianas Islands by the League of Nations. The League of Nations, however, decreed that under no circumstances must Japan militarize any of the islands placed under its trust.

Japan soon violated this restriction by beginning construction of military facilities on some of the islands. Until Amelia Earhart's last flight in 1937, any persons unlucky enough to be caught by the Japanese in their mandated territory, without a good explanation for their presence, were at high risk for execution. Unfortunately, this fate befell some of them.

As Japan's military build-up on their mandated islands increased, so did their fear of being discovered. By 1937, with significant secret fortifications on Truk, Jaluit, and Saipan, among others, Japan was hugely paranoid about anyone who appeared to be penetrating the waters or airspace around these islands. Having learned of Japanese military activities in the mandated islands, the United States and her allies, particularly the British, who had their own interests in the Central Pacific, urgently needed to ascertain the extent of Japanese military fortifications. With the specter of a major war in the near future, intelligence was badly needed.

In 1935, Pan American Airways initiated trans-Pacific flights using Martin M-130 seaplanes, then dubbed "flying boats" to bolster public confidence. This immediately nonplused the Japanese, who did not like the idea of regular flights near or possibly even over their mandated islands. They were particularly concerned because they felt that Pan American routes could be just as easily used by military planes. By 1937, they were apparently beside themselves regarding the now regular and growing flights across the Pacific. There are indications that the Japanese embarked on a campaign of sabotage, disruption and outright attack against both Pan American Airways and the U.S. Government. (See chapter entitled "Dark Agenda.")

The Central Pacific was becoming a very dangerous place.

Earhart, due to her great celebrity and the high esteem in which she was held everywhere, could be expected to go from country to country without difficulty, or arousing suspicion. She could take the occasional clandestine aerial photo and then return to the U.S. without anyone being the wiser.

After Roosevelt and Earhart discussed several alternatives, including mid-air refueling by U.S. military planes, they agreed that an airstrip on Howland Island would be the most practical answer to the aviatrix' need for a mid-Pacific refueling site between the Hawaiian Islands and Lae, New Guinea. Additionally, Earhart's ostensibly civilian flight provided an excellent non-military pretext for the U.S. to build an airstrip on one of their Pacific islands, in an area where militarization by any nation was a touchy matter diplomatically.

Recognizing the strategic importance of the three islands in a possible war and decided to take action, the United States quietly annexed Howland Island, along with Jarvis and Baker Islands in early 1936.

On the recommendation of Secretary of State Cordell Hull, FDR issued a memorandum dated February 19, 1936, instructing State to prepare an order to place the three islands under the trust of the Interior Department. Until then, the British had claimed ownership of the islands. The Secretary of State felt, and the White House agreed, that if they just quietly annexed the islands, this might not be noticed by the British, who had problems of their own just then. This ploy worked.

The judgment of the government as to the strategic value of the islands, especially Howland, was confirmed at the beginning of WWII, when the Japanese, on their way back from attacking Pearl Harbor, viciously attacked Howland Island. The airstrip on the tiny island was destroyed and two of the colonists were killed. The island was rendered useless and the damage was never repaired.

On January 12, 1937, a Coast Guard ship left Honolulu, bound for Howland Island, and carrying the equipment and personnel to build an airstrip. The airstrip was completed barely in time for Earhart's planned takeoff from Luke Field in Hawaii.

There are also indications that at least two other islands, Hull and Canton, were provisioned as alternate landing sites, a standard procedure in such flights. James Donahue found in his investigation that the British had an intelligence presence on Hull Island.

Earhart's flight afforded the perfect pretext for a covert, global, pre-war mapping and reconnaissance effort. And the plan nearly worked. The noted and beloved aviatrix transited smoothly from country to country, rarely being delayed by red tape. She and her navigator, Fred Noonan, usually were expedited through customs wherever they went. And more importantly, Earhart was able to easily take her assigned covert aerial photos throughout most of her flight, especially across the vast and little patrolled wastelands of Central Africa. Until arriving in Lae, New Guinea, the only significant problem Earhart had reportedly encountered was a case of dysentery contracted somewhere in Central Africa.

But in the Central Pacific, the tables would turn. The U.S. Government had seriously underestimated the paranoia and ruthlessness of the Japanese. Given FDR's known fondness for human intelligence, this seems strange, as it is known that the U.S. had several information sources in the area.

One of them was the reports of travelers to or through the Japanese Mandate Islands. Another was a quasi-formal intelligence network in the area in the form of Guamanians, who were allowed by the Japanese to work on their installations on Saipan. When they returned to Guam, they would be debriefed by U.S. officials on their experiences.

As a result, one wonders how the government could have so misjudged the Japanese intentions after years of feedback from their various sources. Since the early 1920s, a number of had demonstrated the extreme danger of impinging on Japanese airspace or waters. Marine Lieutenant Colonel Earl Ellis visited the Caroline Islands in an attempt to gain intelligence. He traveled briefly in the islands and then died there under questionable circumstances on May 12, 1923. Another officer sent to investigate Ellis' death, ended up following the trail to Tokyo, a trail which reportedly led to the infamous Black Dragon Society. Unfortunately, before he could return to make a more complete report, the officer perished in the great earthquake of 1923. A strange affair...

In 1936, Willard Price, a member of the National Geographic Society staff, managed to gain official permission from the Japanese government to visit their Mandated Islands. Amazingly, he was able to stay in the islands for four months. While there, he made many observations which he later reported to the U.S. government, and which provided much information that was useful during WWII. He also encountered intense suspicion and secretiveness on the part of the Japanese, and was only just able to complete his visit in the islands without being arrested by the Japanese. They regularly read his papers and journals and followed him and his wife around. He later wrote a series of famous books, including one on his experiences in the mandated islands entitled "Japan's Islands of Mystery."

Price's observations on Truk, in particular, were controversial, as he insisted that he saw no military installations. However, the U.S. Government's information from its other intelligence sources contradicted Mr. Price's assertions and indicating a military buildup. Also, it is known that the Japanese did their best to conceal their military facilities and made their military personnel dress in civilian clothes. Therefore, it is quite possible that the Japanese were able to successfully fool Price.

Later in the decade, two U.S. naval officers went into the same area on an intelligence mission and were captured by the Japanese. They weren't as lucky as Price and were executed. U.S. authorities later received quiet notification of the executions through diplomatic channels, but given the circumstances, weren't in a position to protest much.

Just before Earhart's flight through the Central Pacific, Japan had begun preparing for an invasion of mainland China, later known as the Second Sino-Japanese War after their invasion on July 7, 1937. Almost all of the Imperial Japanese Navy (IJN) forces were pulled out of the area to support the invasion of China. Unfortunately for Earhart, however, the Japanese had assigned some forces to the area, a move by the Japanese that was far from coincidental.

Ever paranoid about the wrong eyes seeing their secret installations, the Japanese watched the entire Earhart world flight carefully in the media, and lay in vigilant wait, lest she violate their airspace.

When the hapless aviatrix took off from Lae, New Guinea on July 2, 1937, ironically toward the rising sun, she was flying towards the jaws of a waiting dragon.

Author's Collection

Map of the Pacific, ca 1928, source
unknown, except for "John Bartholomew
& Son, Ltd., Edinburgh, Scotland"

Sidebar Mysteries

A Ghost in Garapan Prison?

While some researchers had have eerie experiences, one researcher, Eugene Sims, had one that may have been literally paranormal. In the 1970s, a few years before Buddy Brennan's visits to Saipan, Sims began employment on Guam. As part of his business activities, he began making weekly trips to Saipan.

Sims soon made friends with numerous families on the island, frequently discussing the disappearance of Amelia Earhart with the older members. He soon noticed that few people were comfortable openly discussing the aviatrix' disappearance.

On one visit, Sims brought his wife with him and, as part of a tour of the island, the two were shown Garapan Prison. They were taken to a cell that they were told once held Amelia Earhart. Sims took copious photos of the jail. A few days later, when Sims got the photos back from the processor, he was stunned to see, in one photo of Earhart's cell a ghostly white figure standing in the metal door frame.

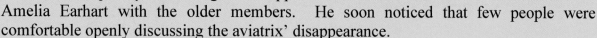

THE KWAJALEIN HOURGLASS

Volume 43, Number 2   Tuesday, January 7, 2003
U.S. Army Kwajalein Atoll, Republic of the Marshall Islands

Records close in protest case

By Jim Bennett
Editor

The contract protests have gone to the jury, of sorts.

The General Accounting Office has closed the records on protests by Raytheon and Northrop Grumman and will issue a decision by Jan. 18 (Kwaj day), according to Guy Pietrovito, the GAO attorney handling the case.

"We're working on a decision," he said. "We don't have one yet."

The GAO is now considering information gathered since the protests were filed Oct. 10 (Kwaj time), including the initial protest documents and subsequent reports, answers to questions and rebuttals to opposing reports. The information gathering process culminated in oral hearings held in Washington D.C. late last month, followed by a final round of reports.

With the case now under deliberation (See CONTRACT, page 5)

Rock solid

(Photo by Jim Bennett)

Lando Cinco, of Dick Pacific Construction, sweeps up aggregate spilled during the unloading process Sunday. Crews will take nine days to unload the 11,000 tons of aggregate, which will be used in the construction of a new cold storage warehouse to be built near the Small Boat Marina. The warehouse should be completed late this year.

Did Amelia Earhart land on Kwajalein Atoll?

By Gene Sims
Special to the Hourglass

At last count I find there have been at least 15 full-length books or novels, more than 30 magazine articles, three full-length movies and innumerable hours of coverage on television and radio about Amelia Earhart, her life and disappearance over the Pacific Ocean in 1937.

Living in Oakland, Calif., in the 1930s as a young teenager, I became one of the millions of Amelia fans after my dad took me to the Oakland airport to see her attempt to be the first person to fly to Hawaii. The flight aborted on the runway because of a landing gear failure, but I can recall vividly the entire incident and the effect it had on my young life. I also remember how disappointed I was when I missed seeing her successful flight from Honolulu and her landing again at the Oakland airport some months later. Amelia was my idol, even if she was a girl.

Our whole family was shocked at her

(Smithsonian Institution Negative #44303a)

Aviatrix Amelia Earhart never completed her round-the-world trip, but she may have visited Kwajalein Atoll.

last flight and disappearance in July 1937. The tragedy was made even closer since our neighbors were some of the family of Fred Noonan, Amelia's navigator on that fateful trip. During my

high school years I carried Amelia's picture with me. Later, in the Navy and then going to Kwajalein near the end of World War II, I was anxious to see the part of the world where Amelia crashed. That experience, and a later quest, was to grow over the years and increase dramatically when I returned to Kwajalein in 1965 with my family.

In 1966, Fred Goerner, the well-known San Francisco CBS radio personality, wrote a book called "The Search for Amelia Earhart." Goerner wrote of his travels to Guam and Saipan in search of information about Amelia's last flight after he read a story about a Guamanian woman who claimed Amelia and Noonan were captured by the Japanese in 1937 and then brought to Saipan. The woman's story appeared in several newspapers and was largely the reason for Goerner being able to convince CBS officials to allow him to investigate further.

(See EARHART, page 4)

www.smdc.army.mil/KWAJ/Hourglass/hourglass.html

Earhart book puts aviatrix in Marshalls ...

(From page 1)

After reading Goerner's book, I reasoned that if the Guamanian woman's story was true, maybe someone else on Kwajalein in 1937 might also have seen Amelia.

During a bull session with a couple of my Marshallese friends one day, I was surprised to hear them speak so openly about the white-skinned lady and man that came to Kwajalein in 1937. One fellow said he was 12 years old in 1937 when his father operated a small fishing boat to catch fish for the Japanese officers mess on Kwajalein. He also recalled helping his father on the boat when he was not in school. One day, he recalled, a large Japanese ship came into the harbor and he saw a white lady and man on the deck. Now, a white woman was a real rarity in that part of the world in 1937, so the event made a lasting impression on the young boy's mind.

When I started asking him details about the woman — her nationality, appearance, etc. — my friend just shrugged his shoulders and said he didn't remember, but he was certain other witnesses still living on Ebeye also knew of the woman.

My further inquiries among the Marshallese on Ebeye produced only second-hand rumors without any concrete facts about seeing Amelia. I continued to collect and read all other written data I could find on her 1937 flight. I read and reread every line of Goerner's book several times.

According to Goerner's findings, Amelia and Fred had landed (crashed?) somewhere on Jaluit or perhaps Mili in the Marshalls. I asked myself why Goerner had never heard or at least reported the story from my Marshallese friend on Kwajalein? I was to find out later he had been denied access to Kwajalein by the Navy. Therein lies the twist of my story.

Had the Navy allowed Goerner access on Kwajalein in early 1960, his findings and his book might have been considerably different. What Goerner was never to learn was concrete proof that Amelia was on Kwajalein and Roi-Namur in 1937.

Much of this proof was based on the testimony of a Jaluit woman named Mera Phillips. She had been the cook and interpreter for an American lady captured by the Japanese and held prisoner on Roi in 1937.

The Mera Phillips story was further confirmed in 1993 by statements from John Tobeke, a Marshallese working on Roi. Tobeke stated that when he was about 6 years old and living on Roi, he saw a white woman and man twice over a period of three months. In addition to the testimony he gave to Neal

Eugene C. Sims

Proctor, an instructor from the University of Maryland who was visiting Kwajalein, Tobeke was shown pictures of three different white women. He successfully identified the picture of Amelia as the woman he had seen while a child on Roi in 1937.

The story of this interview by Jane Toma appeared in the Dec. 15, 1993, edition of the Kwajalein Hourglass.

In the Hourglass story, Toma also tells of the finding of a pilot's leather flight bag in the debris of a Japanese airplane hangar on Roi sometime after the takeover of the island in February 1944. The bag was embossed in gold leaf with the letters "A.E." and was thought to belong to Amelia Earhart. More on this story can be read in "The Roi-Namur Kwajalein Atoll Historical Guide" as published by KREMS.

For reasons I never understood, the military kept the briefcase find secret until a few years ago, when it became public and appeared in the Honolulu Advertiser and several other newspapers.

In 1972 I was transferred to Agana, Guam, to set up a new business for Global Associates. My wife and I remained on Guam for more than eight years and during that time I continued to learn more about the fate of Amelia Earhart.

As an engineer and manager of the new business, I was required to travel extensively throughout Micronesia. I also made weekly trips to Saipan, where I became friends with many of the island's indigenous families. Some of these friends had resided on Saipan in the 1930s and the subject of Amelia Earhart was discussed many times with older residents. I found that few people wished to discuss the 1937 event or her appearance in Saipan.

My wife and me were shown various places on Saipan where Amelia allegedly had been seen. One man took me to a spot in the old cemetery, where he claimed Amelia was buried. But the most interesting place we visited was the old Garapan prison used by the Japanese in the 1930s. After the American forces recaptured Saipan in mid-1944, the old stone-and-steel-framed prison building was abandoned and left to decay.

Our guide showed us the jail cells where Amelia and Fred were supposedly held captive. I took many pictures. Several days later after the pictures had been developed, I was shocked to see one print of Amelia's cell. In the rusted metal frame of the cell door stood a white, ghostly figure. Was this some sort of photo misprint? I had the picture reprinted and again the ghostly outline was evident.

I considered the ghost to be a message from Amelia, and put my collection of the aviatrix in my locked files. What good would it do to show the picture?

This last year, after my wife's passing, I made a move to a new, smaller home. It was clear I needed to clean out boxes of various written materials collected over almost 50 years. I uncovered the Amelia files and for several weeks I reread the voluminous data on her life.

At first, I reasoned the information might make a whale of a story, but then realized maybe the data would just become more controversy about the fate of Amelia Earhart and Fred Noonan. At this time, I have no intention of writing anything more on the subject. My files are closed, but I still look at that ghostly picture and wonder.

Let Amelia and Fred rest in peace. Amen.

(Editor's Note: Gene Sims is the unofficial historian of Kwajalein Atoll, author of Kwajalein Remembered, a collection of reminiscences of life at Kwaj and contributor to the Hourglass. Sims was stationed here in 1945 with the Navy and returned on two subsequent tours as a civilian, 1964-71 and 1983-86.)

Above, views of the interior
of Garapan Prison on Saipan

Thinking the photo to be some sort of laboratory error, Sims had another print made. It came out exactly the same. In an article in the *Kwajalein Hourglass*, Sims reminisced that as far as he was concerned, the image was a message from Earhart.

It used to be that Saipan was a restricted area that couldn't be visited without permission. This was because the U.S. government was operating an espionage training facility on the north end of the island and understandably required some security. Following the release of Fred Goerner's book in 1966, the U.S. government shut shown its sensitive facilities and the island reverted to a peace that hadn't been known since before the Japanese occupation. Nowadays, ironically, people are encouraged to visit the island, as it is a tourist stop. Garapan Prison has been rescued from the jungle, and reportedly, everyday at noon, an Earhart impersonator comes out of the building to give a performance for the visitors.

Had Gene Sims captured the restless spirit of the long-missing aviatrix on film? And what could she have been trying to tell him?

Notes in a Bottle

Another strange side-mystery in the disappearance of Amelia Earhart started the day before Halloween 1938 near Soulac-Sur-Mer, France. On October 30, 1938, a Mrs. Genevieve Barrat, aged 37, was walking on the beach near the town and noticed a small bottle floating near the shore. Retrieving the bottle, Mme Barrat noticed its caacity was about eight ounces, that it was closed with a cork and sealed with wax.

In the bottle she found a lock of hair and three documents. Written in French, the first document contained only the words, "God guide this bottle. I confide my life and that of my companions to it." The second document, also in French, was considerably longer and covered both sides of the paper. The third document was in shorthand.

Mme Barrat immediately took the bottle and its contents to the local police (Gendarmes), who, after reviewing the materials, sent them on through channels, until they finally arrived at the National Gendarmerie headquarters in Paris (See copy of National Gendarmerie report in Appendix IV.) The French authorities eventually notified the U.S. State Department, which, ultimately, took no significant action. Their copies of the material ended up in the U.S. National Archives.

The beach at Soulac Sur Mer

Below follows the complete text of the notes:

"Have been prisoner at Jaluit (Marshall) of Japanese in a prison at Jaluit. Have seen Amelia Earhart (aviatrix) and in another prison her mechanic (man), as well as other prisoners; held for so-called espionage of gigantic fortifications which are built at Atoll.

"Earhart and her companion were picked up by a Japanese seaplane and will be held as hostages, say the Japanese. I was a prisoner because I debarked at Mili Atoll. My yacht 'Viveo' sunk, crew massacred (3 Maoris), the boat (26 T) was supplied with wireless.

On the reverse of the paper:

"Having remained a long time at Jaluit as prisoner, I was enrolled by force as a bunker-hand on board 'Nippon Nom?' going to for Europe. Shall escape as soon as the ship is near the coast. Take this message immediately to the Gendarmerie in order that we may be saved.

This message was probably thrown off Santander, and will surely arrive at the Vendee towards September or at the least October 1938, remainder in the bottle tied to this one, Message No. 6."

A third document, in shorthand, read:

"In order to have more chance of freeing Miss Amelia Earhart and her companion, as well as the other prisoners, it would be preferable that policemen should arrive incognito at Jaluit. I shall be with JO . . . eux and if I succeed in escaping . . . for if the Japanese are asked to free the prisoners, they will say that they have no prisoners at Jaluit. It will therefore be necessary to be craft in order to save the prisoners of Jaluit. At the risk of my life, I shall send further messages.

"This bottle serves as a float for a second bottle containing the story of my life and . . . empty, and a few objects having belonged to Amelia Earhart. These documents prove the truth of the story in ordinary writing and shorthand and that I have approached Amelia Earhart . . . believed to be dead.

"The second bottle doesn't matter.

"I am writing on my knees for I have only a little paper, for fingerprints taken by the police. Another with thumb.

"Message written on the cargo board, No. 6."

The second bottle was never found, and the anonymous writer of the notes was never identified.

South African investigator Oliver Knaggs later carried out a thorough investigation of the notes after he discovered copies of them in a microfilm roll he had obtained from the U.S. National Archives.

The notes were sandwiched in among numerous bizarre notes and communications received by the U.S. government in the 1930s. Subsequently, he mounted a lengthy trip to France, the United States and Guam to investigate the disappearance of Amelia Earhart.

Oddly, just before Knaggs and his wife left on their trip, Knaggs' briefcase was stolen. It contained Knagg's correspondence file which he and his wife and carefully assembled for the trip, as well as all of the contact information and notes they would need for the trip, along with the microfilm Knaggs had gotten from the U.S. National Archives. Was this just a chance theft—or did someone want to impede Knaggs investigation?

Undaunted, Knaggs and his wife proceeded with their trip as planned.

Knaggs later detailed his investigation in his now difficult to find book, "Amelia Earhart: Her Last Flight." He was able during his trip to view all the materials in the French archives in Paris, as well as in the U.S. National Archives.

After he had reviewed the evidence, Knaggs carefully thought things over and made a list of "pros" and "cons" regarding the authenticity of the materials in the bottle.

Favoring the document's authenticity, for Knaggs, were a number of factors. Knaggs first cited the evident knowledge of South Pacific geography and of Japanese fortifications on some of them. Second, Knaggs felt the lock of hair found in the bottle may have been authentic, for although the report written in Paris in January 1939 at the Brigade level cited the color of the hair as "chestnut", the Gendarmerie Report described the hair as "light brown." Knaggs also found the writer's remarks describing Earhart as an aviatrix and Noonan as "her mechanic" to be so seemingly uninformed and unaffected that they almost had to be a mark of credibility. Also, the writer's reference to having been arrested because he had simply disembarked at Mili seemed credible in light of later hindsight about the Japanese fortification of that area. "How on earth could anyone have made such a statement unless he had been there?" Knaggs asks in his book.

Knaggs mentioned in his book that he had located a Monsieur Eric De Bisschop, a former French naval officer, who had, during a trip through the South Pacific in 1938 been briefly detained by the Japanese. According to Bisschop, his initial reception had been quite cordial until he mentioned that he had passed close to Mili Atoll. Abruptly, all friendliness evaporated, and he was placed under arrest. He was crisply interrogated for several hours, but finally released after the Japanese could find no evidence of espionage activities.

Against the authenticity of the materials in the bottle, Knaggs noted several things. First of all was the fact that the writer did not give his name, although Knaggs conceded that the writer may have feared the bottle would fall into the wrong hands. The next negative factor that concerned Knaggs was the method of delivery: a sealed bottle washed up on a beach. This was definitely a rather melodramatic method of receiving such a disclosure. Finally, Knaggs listed as a negative factor the lock of hair found in the bottle. He admitted that he had listed it as a "con" because he realized that, since he had not been able to see the actual lock of hair, its color could be argued either way.

In the end, Knaggs was fairly well convinced of the authenticity of the messages in the bottle. But frustratingly, he had been unable to locate the actual bottle or the lock of hair for examination.

Again, we are left with another strange tale with no final resolution. It is a tale filled with enough corroboratable information to be tantalizing but not conclusive.

Is there any truth to the strange notes and lock of hair once found in a bottle on seashore in France?

Tokyo Rose

Iva Ikuko Toguri D'Aquino

Amelia Earhart

Another strange facet of Amelia Earhart's disappearance was the rumor that arose during WWII regarding "Tokyo Rose." "Tokyo Rose" was the pseudonym of a series of women who made numerous radio broadcasts in the Pacific Theater of Operations during WWII. The broadcasts were designed to disseminate misinformation and demoralize allied troops in the Pacific area.

By 1944, the rumor had surfaced that none other than the missing aviatrix Amelia Earhart was the voice behind the broadcasts. George Palmer Putnam, who had been commissioned a major in the Army Intelligence Corps in 1942, was serving on a bomber base in the Burma area. Thus, when the government decided to send him to monitor the Tokyo Rose broadcasts, it was an easy matter. Putnam was sent to a Marine Corps radio station in a Japanese occupied area of China, ostensibly so that he would be as close as possible to the transmission source of the Tokyo Rose broadcasts. His mission was to listen to several Tokyo Rose broadcasts to determine if in fact the voice was that of his former wife, Amelia Earhart. After listening to a single broadcast, for less than a minute, GP exclaimed, "I'll stake my life that that is not Amelia's voice. It sounds to me as if the woman might have lived in New York, and of course, she had been fiendishly well coached, but Amelia—never!"

A new perspective regarding G. P. Putnam's trip to China arose just before this author completed LEGERDEMAIN As mentioned earlier in this book, I had occasion to meet with Amelia Earhart researcher Ron Bright, and among the subjects discussed was Putnam's trip to China. Ron surprised me a little by mentioning to me that his research showed that the only source for the account of GP's trip was Muriel Earhart Morrisey. Thus, he told me, he doubted the provenance of the report and felt that it may never have happened.

Could this well-known anecdote be a fiction? That is up to the reader, although, with no solid evidence discrediting the account of GP's trip, this writer sees no reason not to continue to give credence to it.

Another odd aspect of GP's foray behind the lines in China is that it wasn't really necessary to go to such a dangerous area to listen to the radio broadcasts. In short, Putnam could have listened to them almost anywhere in the Asian theatre of operations.

A complicating factor in the Tokyo Rose matter was that more than one voice had appeared over radio as Tokyo Rose. As a result, it is impossible to say how many different women lent their voices to the effort.

In the summer of 1949, the U.S. decided that a Japanese-American named Iva Ikuko Toguri D'Aquino was Tokyo Rose, and they put her on trial in San Francisco. Despite the fact that the defense produced evidence that up to fifteen different women were involved in the broadcasts, the court found D'Aquino guilty on one of the eight counts. She was sentenced to ten years and was released six years later, with time off for good behavior.

Another strange aspect to the Tokyo Rose mystery is that many of the eyewitnesses on Saipan who reported seeing Earhart after her capture said that residents of the island habitually referred to the woman captive as "Tokyo Rosa." When questioned by Joe Gervais in the 1960s, one Antonio M. Cepada mentioned this fact.

"Why do you call her that?" Gervais queried.

"Everyone on Saipan referred to her as Tokyo Rosa. In 1937, Tokyo Rosa meant American spy lady."

"You mean Tokyo Rose on the Japanese radio during the war? That Tokyo Rose?" Gervais asked in surprise.

"Not that one", Cepada said, shaking his head.

"Tokyo Rosa in 1937 meant American spy girl. That's all. Nothing else."

Recent research on this author's part has turned up the repeated assertion in numerous quarters that the name of Tokyo Rose was never actually heard on any of the broadcasts and was a nickname applied to those broadcasts by American GIs.

GP Putnam and his son David shortly After their induction in 1942

As a postscript to the affair, Iva Ikuko Toguri D'Aquino was later given a Presidential Pardon by Gerald Ford in the 1970s. There is currently a movement on to ask the Congress to refund to Ms. D'Aquino the $10,000 fine she originally paid the government and award her a Congressional Pardon. One can only hope that Ms. D'Aquino, will receive the long overdue justice she deserves while she is still alive.

It's possible that the name for the Tokyo Rose affair may have had its genesis in the prewar years in the South Pacific, from the slang "Tokyo Rosa" reported Earhart witnesses. Perhaps GIs who invaded some of the islands picked up that local slang a applied it later to the Japanese radio broadcasts.

Ultimately, the whole affair could be discarded if it were not for a couple of troubling issues. T first is that there are indications that U.S. Army G-2 (Intelligence) seriously thought in 1944 tl Amelia Earhart was behind the so-called Tokyo Rose broadcasts. And as we have seen, t government took the rumors seriously enough to apparently send GP into a combat zone to investiga them.

Second, it seems quite eerie that both the phrase "Tokyo Rose" and "Tokyo Rosa", would have t single common denominator of Amelia Earhart. Is there some further significant aspect to the Tok Rose affair, which has yet to be identified, much less plumbed?

Crash at Bicycle Lake – A Mystery Solved – or Was It?

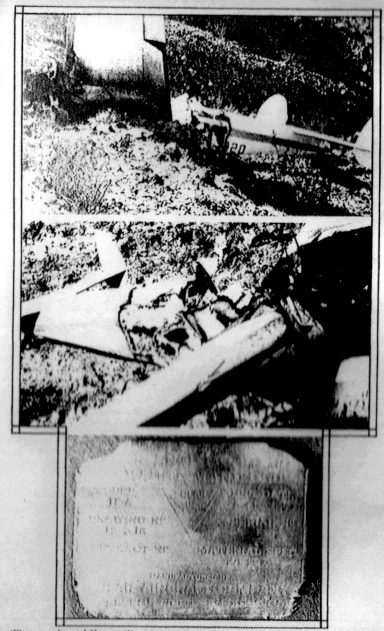

(Top and middle) Official F.A.A. photos taken on the California mountainside which clearly show the registration N-16020, the same as that of the Lockheed Electra of Amelia's last flight. (Bottom) The exhaust manifold plate found in the above wreckage. Note the delivery date, May 5, 1937.

Above illustration from AMELIA EARHART LIVES, by Joseph Klaas and Joseph Gervais

On the evening of December 15, 1961, a group of civilian and military pilots attended the annual Lockheed pilots' party at the Palmdale Country Club in California. Later in the evening, many of the pilots began to swap stories of daring-do and soon challenges to perform even more daring deeds began to pass between them. At approximately midnight, a group of eight pilots left for nearby Quartz Hill Airport, where two of their group, Charles Kitchens and Braxton Harrell, had decided to take off on an impromptu flight to Las Vegas. The aircraft in question was a Lockheed Electra.

Kitchens, was the head of a three-man *consortium* that had purchased the Lockheed ship on February 14th of that year from Paul Mantz, Amelia Earhart's technical advisor. The craft was later described by a mechanic appeared to have not more than 500 hours total [flying] time. It had seen a lot of storage in its day."

At 3:00 a.m. on December 16, 1961, the Lockheed Electra flew over the Bicycle Lake Army who worked at the hangar as being the…. "most beautiful Electra I had ever seen. Not a scratch or dent on it. It Airbase and made a turn to the left, evidently getting into pattern to land on Runway 22, which was lighted and available. A moment later, at 3:01 a.m., the beautiful, mint condition craft was observed by base personnel to hit the side of nearby Mt. Tierfort, explode, and burst into flames.

The ensuing official investigation revealed that the port (left) engine had failed, causing a serious power loss and making it impossible for the crew of the ship to avoid hitting the mountainside. The report also indicated that this aircraft did not have fully-feathering propellers, an important feature in making a safe emergency landing.

Coincidentally, neither did Amelia Earhart's Electra, as fully-feathering and constant speed propellers were not introduced on Lockheed aircraft until September 1937, shortly after Earhart's disappearance.

Subsequently, Major Joseph Gervais, who had been conducting his own investigation into the disappearance of Amelia Earhart, "Operation Earhart," learned of the crash. Securing the permission of the base commander of Fort Irwin, the reservation on which Bicycle Lake AAB was located, Gervais climbed Mt. Tierfort to inspect the crash site. An experienced aircraft crash investigator, Major Gervais was well qualified for this task.

At the crash scene, Gervais found that some pieces of the Electra still remained. Strangely, identifying plates of all sorts had been carefully removed from the wreckage. However, part of the CAA registration number survived on an undamaged portion of the fuselage. Gervais took photos of this. Then, Gervais began searching further from the main crash site, having been taught by his crash investigation experience that other pieces of an aircraft are usually thrown some distance from the impact site.

A hundred yards from the main impact site, in a rocky ravine, Gervais found three sections of exhaust manifold, which represented parts of both airplane engines. Using a hammer and chisel, he broke open the cowlings and discovered that the identification plates for the manifolds were intact.

Each plate was stamped: "Exhaust Manifold manufactured by Solar Aircraft Corp., Lindbergh Field, San Diego, California. Model 12. Delivery Date May 13, 1937." Gervais determined that the crashed ship was a Lockheed Electra Model 12A, Serial No. 1243, FAA Registration No. N16020, the same number assigned to the Lockheed aircraft flown by Amelia Earhart during her last flight.

What was so significant about this crash was that the aircraft bore the federal aircraft registration number of Amelia Earhart's Lockheed, N16020. According to the history books, this crash could not have happened--this craft was supposed to have disappeared in the Central Pacific in 1937. If N16020 did not go down with Amelia Earhart in 1937, how did it end up on a hilltop in California in 1961?

Subsequent research by Joseph Gervais and others established that the plane had been purchased quietly by Paul Mantz in 1946 to use in a film about Amelia Earhart. As part of his preparations, Mantz had secured the permission of the FAA to use Earhart's old aircraft ID number. Subsequently, Mantz sold the plane to a private company in 1961.

The remaining puzzle is why Mantz purchased the plane in an odd three phase non-sequential transaction from a company that did not at the time own the plane.

The Mystery of Irene Bolam

Guy and Irene Bolam, 1965

During the final phase of Joe Gervais' investigation, Operation Earhart, events continued to take strange turns. In the summer of 1965, Gervais received a letter from Viola Gentry, a friend of his aunt, inviting him and his wife to a special luncheon in their honor given by the Early Flyers Club. The meeting was to be held at the West Hampton Air Force Base and Major Gervais was scheduled to make a presentation to the club members regarding Operation Earhart. Miss Gentry promised Gervais that many of Amelia Earhart's old friends would be there. Gervais cheerfully accepted the invitation, little realizing the experience awaiting him.

On the day of the luncheon, Gervais and his wife met Viola Gentry in a large banquet room at the Sea Spray on the Dunes in East Hampton. Gervais had brought along a camera loaded with color film and was happily snapping photos of various old-time aviation figures like a sightseer as he strolled around the room.

Just then, Viola Gentry, who had been looking toward the nearby sea, turned back to look into the room and stopped to stare. Across the room, a silver-haired man and woman had entered through a door.

"Why, there's Irene Bolam", Viola said in awe. "It really is Mrs. Bolam."

Gervais glanced in the same direction and froze. The woman Viola Gentry had called Irene Bolam had a stunning resemblance to Amelia Earhart. After spending years of examining photos and film clips of Earhart, Gervais was almost thunderstruck. In fact, he immediately wondered if he were looking at a 68 year old Amelia Earhart.

Keeping his voice almost to a whisper, Gervais asked Miss Gentry with a stammer, "Viola, could I please meet that woman?"

"Oh yes", Miss Gentry replied. "You must meet Mrs. Bolam."

Miss Gentry led Gervais over to Mr. and Mrs. Bolam and introduced them to the air force officer. Gervais couldn't get over the deja vu-like feeling that he knew or had known Mrs. Bolam.

"I'm most delighted to meet you, Mrs. Bolam", Gervais said. "Were you a friend of Amelia Earhart?"

"Yes", Mrs. Bolam said quietly with a distant smile. "I knew her."

"I'll bet you knew Amelia rather well."

"Yes, I knew her rather well", Mrs. Bolam said, an enigmatic twinkle in her eyes. Pinned to her dress were several medals. Joe Gervais indicated in his book that they were a miniature Distinguished Flying Cross, (which can only be worn by those who have been awarded it), a miniature of the medal awarded to Amelia Earhart by New York for her transatlantic flight, and a miniature major's oak leaf cluster. Unfortunately it is hard to tell from the photo he took if this is correct.

"Were you a pilot, Mrs. Bolam?" Gervais asked.

"Oh, yes", she replied softly.

"Did you ever fly with Amelia Earhart?", Gervais continued.

"Yes, Major. I flew with Amelia", Mrs. Bolam said.

At this point, Gervais began talking with Mr. Bolam, suddenly afraid of appearing too obvious.

Near the end of the conversation, Gervais asked Mrs. Bolam for her address so that he might write to her some time. After exchanging looks with her husband, Mrs. Bolam gave Major Gervais a card with her address on it.

Gervais then stepped back from the couple and asked if he could take a picture. Mrs. Bolam started to protest and then Gervais snapped the shutter.

"Just one", Gervais said. "I'll send you a copy."

Irene Bolam stared in confusion at her husband. Viola Gentry gasped and Guy Bolam shrugged.

"Oh, well, I suppose just one", Mr. Bolam conceded.

"Are you a Ninety-Nine?" Gervais then asked Mrs. Bolam, to which she replied "Yes." He also asked her if she was a member of the Zontas, a feminists' sorority to which Amelia Earhart had belonged. Mrs. Bolam again replied in the affirmative.

At that point, Guy Bolam abruptly made an excuse and he and Mrs. Bolam moved to another part of the room.

After lunch, Gervais gave a talk about Project Earhart. At the conclusion, there was a brief surprise ceremony in which his wife was presented with the Amelia Earhart Award for Outstanding Contribution to Research in the History of Aviation, for her assistance to her husband in Operation Earhart. Gervais noted that Mr. and Mrs. Bolam had left before his talk.

That evening after Gervais had returned to his hotel room, he received a call from Irene Bolam, inviting him and his wife to her home the following evening. When Gervais asked the nature of the invitation, Mrs. Bolam told him she wished to discuss his investigation into the disappearance of Amelia Earhart. Gervais had to decline the invitation because he had to pick up his children the next day from a relative's home and had airline seats reserved for the next day.

He would later realize that declining Irene Bolam's invitation was one of the biggest mistakes he ever made, as he spent the rest of Operation Earhart trying to get in contact with Mrs. Bolam. She failed to keep every appointment which she subsequently made with Gervais.

After the Long Island luncheon, Gervais and Klaas made repeated attempts to check Irene Bolam's background, finally writing a letter to Mrs. Bolam asking her to provide proof of her identity so that they could follow other leads if they were wrong.

Mrs. Bolam wrote them back, giving Gervais' friend, Viola Gentry, as a reference, as well as one Elmo Pickerill of New York State. Viola Gentry sent a fairly brief note back to Gervais, but Mr. Pickerill sent a more extensive letter detailing Mrs. Bolam's background.

Unfortunately, Klaas and Gervais could find no independent source with which to verify the information in Mr. Pickerill's letter. A query to the FAA Records Center in Oklahoma City, brought the response that a student's license had been issued to Irene Bolam under her previous married name, Craigmile, (no number), on 9-20-32 and a private license, #28958, on 5-27-33 .

Subsequently, Gervais and Klaas requested a copy of Mrs. Craigmile's pilot licenses and were sent a copy of a non-commercial pilot's license, #28958, dated 5-31-37. The date had been crossed out and penciled in above it was 6-1-37. The address given for Mrs. Craigmile was in Brooklyn, NY and the license was unsigned.

Clearly, the copy of the license contradicted the information the FAA had given Gervais in their first letter. Why would such a contradiction exist? Was this evidence of a cover-up?

One new possibility that has surfaced among researchers is that in the spring of 1937, Irene Craigmile's 1933 license was about to expire and the 5-31-37 license may have been automatically issued, as a matter of course. Or that it had been issued in error.

If the license was automatically issued, in contemplation of Mrs. Craigmile showing up to claim it, the timing is remarkably coincidental. For the document was dated the day AE departed from Miami on her world flight. Moreover, by 1937, Mrs. Craigmile had married Alvin Heller (see Ron Reuther's timeline in Appendix I) and any replacement license should have been changed long before to the name Irene Heller. Why was the 1937 license issued to Irene Craigmile under that name?

The whole matter of Irene Craigmile Bolam's flying licenses is far from clear.

Gervais and Klaas wrote another letter to Mrs. Bolam, this time asking her about not only her past, but the purpose of Earhart's last flight, and Wilbur Rothar as well (See chapter on Wilbur Rothar). They never received an answer to that letter.

76

Much later, in one of Gervais' last telephone contacts with Irene Bolam, she made some telling remarks. After Gervais implored her to arrange an appointment for them to talk, Mrs. Bolam said, "Oh, I can't see you in this country."

"I beg your pardon?" Gervais replied.

"I mean, I couldn't meet with you in the United States. Look, Major Gervais. I once had a public life. I once had a career in flying. But I've retired. I've given that all up now. As a major retired from the air force, you should be able to understand this." She made an appointment to meet Gervais at a hotel in Montreal, which she didn't keep, to Gervais' frustration.

Subsequently, after Gervais had returned to his home in Las Vegas, Viola Gentry flew there from the East Coast. The next day, Gervais had dinner with Miss Gentry and two other persons in a Las Vegas restaurant.

"Irene has gone to Paris. You'll never see her again", Miss Gentry told Gervais. Ironically, Gervais and Klaas would indeed see Irene Bolam again one day, in open court.

"You know, Viola", Gervais said at length "there are a lot of people interested in this case. It could be worth a lot of money to find out what happened out there on July 2, 1937."

Nodding, Miss Gentry said "That's what Amelia says."

Everyone at the table stopped talking and stared at Viola.

"Viola, do you realize what you just said?" Gervais asked softly.

"What?" Miss Gentry said.

"You said that's what Amelia *says*. As if she were alive."

"Oh, my. Did I say that?" Miss Gentry said. "I meant Muriel. You know. . . Amelia's sister. Muriel Morrissey. I often confuse their names."

After that, Joe Gervais was never able to speak with Irene Bolam again. And, interestingly, when he checked with the Ninety-Nines and the Zontas, he was told that the name Irene Bolam was not on their membership lists.

Left and below,. articles from the October 18-29 1982 series in the Woodbridge, N J News Tribune; above, an upset Irene Bolam at a news conference in1972.

Thinking about it recently, this writer had one thought: The membership lists of the two old-time aviation clubs may not have included the name of Irene Bolam, but there was one way Mrs. Bolam could have been a member of those two clubs. Their lists did include the name of Amelia Earhart . . .

One strange postscript to the Bolam affair was the result of the lawsuit she later filed against Mr. Klaas and Mr. Gervais when *Amelia Earhart Lives* was published. When the suit reached court in 1975, the court asked Mrs. Bolam to give her fingerprints to the court in front of the judge to confirm her identity and settle the matter. This she declined to do. According to recent information from Joe Klaas, the court then recommended to Irene Bolam's attorney that perhaps they ought to negotiate a settlement over the case with McGraw-Hill's attorneys.

What happened was a confidential settlement between McGraw-Hill and Irene Bolam, with Klaas and Gervais having no further involvement in the case. They were even indemnified, according to Joe Klaas, from further lawsuits by Irene Bolam. Shortly afterward, she moved to Paris, France.

Yet another strange postscript to the Bolam affair was an investigation conducted by screenwriter Tod Swindell in 2002. Swindell arranged for two forensic pathologists to use the recent technology of photo superimposition.

In this case, photos of Amelia Earhart and Mrs. Bolam were superimposed over each other and then closely studied to determine whether the bone structure coincided or not. After comparing the bone structure in Mrs. Bolam's face and hands with those of Amelia Earhart, the pathologists concluded that the bone structure coincided exactly.

John Bolam, half brother of Mrs. Bolam's husband, Guy Bolam, stated at first that "we were inclined to think Irene probably was not Amelia Earhart." "However", he went on, "the forensic studies are very convincing." Bolam also stated that while Mrs. Bolam denied being Amelia Earhart, she was not an ordinary housewife as she claimed. "She was influential, knew many well-placed people and was well-traveled."

In the end, one is left to wonder, in light of the above, why Mrs. Bolam, wanting to keep her real identity, whatever it was, confidential, would have subjected herself to the publicity of a lawsuit. It is a mystery that only time may solve.

Top row, three images from Tod Swindell's study, L to R, Amelia Earhart, Irene Bolam and Amelia Earhart superimposed over Irene Bolam; Bottom row, a series of images in overlay by David Deal from Irene Bolam to Amelia Earhart

The Rothar Affair

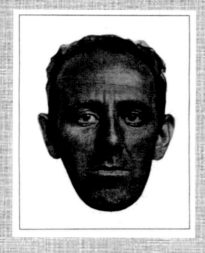

Following the disappearance of Amelia Earhart, a strange series of events occurred in August 1937, which remain one of the most remarkable features of the Earhart disappearance, and may also contain important clues as well.

On July 25, 1937, newspapers reported that Sydney S. Bowman, head of the Pan Pacific Press Bureau and close friend of George Putnam, had posted a $2000 reward on Putnam's behalf the previous day. This was for information "which would definitely clear up the mystery surrounding the disappearance of Amelia Earhart and Fred Noonan." Bowman was quoted as saying the reward would be paid for the "recovery and delivery of any part of the Earhart plane or its contents, which may be identified and which would clearly reveal the fate of the missing flyers."

This convoluted statement sounded as if an attorney had written it.

"There is a chance that further investigation may disclose information upon which absolute conclusions may be reached", Bowman went on. "It is regarded as possible that ships operating in the south Pacific may come upon evidence that would end speculation regarding the aviatrix and her navigator, and it is to encourage this cooperation that the reward has been offered."

On August 5, 1937, a story appeared in the New York Times: "Janitor is Seized for Earhart Hoax." The article reported that several days before, on Saturday, George Putnam had received a strange note, which had been left for him at the Hotel Barclay. The Barclay was a place Putnam regularly stayed when in town. The note read: "We have your wife on the ship. I will call Sunday at 2 o'clock."

About 10:00 p.m. the same day, Putnam received a telephone call from a man, telling him that if he would arrange for a meeting the next day, Sunday, he would receive important information about Amelia Earhart. A meeting was promptly set for Sunday at 2:00 p.m. in Putnam's hotel room.

At 2:00 p.m. the next day, Wilbur Rothar reportedly showed up at the Hotel Barclay to tell Putnam an astonishing tale. Introducing himself as Mr. Johnson, Rothar then told the publisher that he had been employed on a vessel, which was running guns to Spain. The vessel was traveling from New Guinea to Panama. Several days out of New Guinea, the ship anchored off of a small island to take on a fresh water supply.

In a cove on this island, according to Rothar, the landing party from the ship spotted a crashed airplane. Nearby, was a woman who was delirious and very ill, staggering along the shore. According to Rothar, the woman was wearing only a pair of shorts. On the wing of the plane lay the body of a man who had been killed by sharks. Rothar said that the woman was taken aboard the ship and treated by the ship's Chinese doctor during the remainder of their voyage.

When the ship reached Panama, according to Rothar, they recognized the woman from newspapers as Amelia Earhart. They flew into a panic because they were afraid their illegal activities would be discovered if they tried to put Earhart ashore for help.

The ship then continued to New York, Rothar said, and he was elected by fellow crewmembers to approach Putnam. Rothar stressed that many of the men aboard the ship were "cutthroats" and had talked repeatedly about dumping Earhart into the sea. He indicated that Ms. Earhart was so ill that she would have to be taken off the ship and to a hospital soon.

Putnam then requested proof of the story and Rothar said he had proof and would appear at Mr. Putnam's office the next day with it. On Monday, Rothar appeared in Putnam's office with a scarf, which Putnam's secretary recognized as belonging to Amelia Earhart. Rothar stated that the crew had definitely decided that they would not release Earhart unless they were paid the $2000 reward

Putnam said he would happily pay the reward and asked Rothar to come back the next day for the money. The next day, Rothar again appeared in Putnam's office and was given $1000 in cash. While he was at a bank cashing a check for the other $1000, Rothar was arrested. Rothar reportedly confessed to trying to commit a fraud on Putnam. Authorities were reported to have discovered that Rothar was a janitor from the Bronx and the father of eight children.

Rothar later told authorities that he had gotten the scarf some three years earlier at a Long Island airport, when he had gone there to try to get a glimpse of Earhart. As Earhart got into her plane, the media reported, the scarf fell to the ground and Rothar retrieved it. Rothar reportedly said that he had kept the scarf as a memento.

Joe Gervais investigated this incident as part of Operation Earhart, and was very interested in the incident due to its strangeness. A short time after Rothar's arrest he was arraigned and ordered sent to Bellevue Hospital in New York for ten days observation. Two months later, on October 13 1937, Rothar was committed to the Matteawan State Hospital for the Criminally Insane, pending trial on the extortion charge.

From painstaking checking of records, Gervais found that Rothar remained institutionalized for the next 24 years—and was never tried for anything! This seemed a strange outcome for a run-of-the-mill extortion charge.

Interestingly, after various investigations into Earhart's disappearance began to get publicity in 1960, Rothar, now listed as Wilbur Rokar, was transferred from Matteawan State Hospital to Harlem Valley State Hospital on April 19, 1960.

On March 23, 1962, Rokar was transferred to Central Islip State Hospital. In October 1962, he escaped from that facility and remained at large for a year. The following year, he was returned to that hospital and a short time later, on October 2, 1963, Rokar was officially discharged, never to be heard of again.

Muriel Morrissey, Amelia Earhart's sister, recounted the above incident very differently. She maintained that the amount of money that Rothar demanded was $5000 and that the scarf, which Rothar presented to GP, had been found by him in Hawaii, possibly in March 1937. She characterized Rothar as a "shamefaced and frightened young man", as opposed to the 42-year-old father of eight, which the media reported Rothar to be. She said that GP did not prosecute Rothar, exclaiming to Rothar that his wife would not even let him discharge a member of his household staff for starting a kitchen fire. According to Mrs. Morrissey, GP gave the man $50 for the scarf and admonished him to mend his ways in the future.

Held as Extorter in Earhart 'Rescue'

Wilbur Rothar, above, Bronx, N. Y., handyman, was arrested on charges of extortion after he allegedly attempted to obtain $2000 from George Palmer Putnam, her husband, for revealing the whereabouts of Amelia Earhart, who, he said, had been taken safely off a South Seas Island by a smuggling ship on which he was a sailor. Rothar hasn't been to sea in 22 years.

The reality of what happened was that shortly after Rothar was arrested, G. P. Putnam was present in court to press charges against the hapless janitor.

In her book, *Whistled Like a Bird,* Sally Putnam Chapman, the granddaughter of G. P. Putnam recounted essentially the same scenario as Mrs. Morrissey.

Joe Gervais was never able to find evidence that Wilbur Rothar had ever existed. When he traced down the address for Mr. Rothar, which had been published in the newspaper, he found that the address was non-existent, and would have been somewhere at the bottom of the East River . . .

In a further search for information, I discovered that in 1940 an article had been published in *True Detective Magazine* regarding the Rothar affair, and was able to locate a copy of that issue. The article reveals other details that at once both deepen the mystery and suggest a solution. The first thing I noticed was that Rothar's name had transformed from "Wilbur" to "Wilber." Also, in this article, Rothar claimed that he wasn't engaged in smuggling arms, but engaged in "dope-running" aboard a "fast freighter." In addition, further details were reported regarding Earhart's attire.

"She didn't have a thing on", Rothar told Putnam with some embarrassment, "except…"

"Except what?" Putnam prompted.

81

"Why, just some underwear", Rothar said hesitantly.

"What kind?" Putnam persisted.

"Well, it wasn't the kind women wear", Rothar said.

"What kind, men's?" Putnam asked. "Go on, describe the shorts."

"Why, there's nothing much to describe", Rothar said. "Just little, tight-fitting cotton things. There's a name for them." He paused for a moment, then said, "Oh, I know. Jockey shorts."

Putnam was reportedly shocked because he had indeed purchased some jockey shorts for his wife just before she left on her last flight. "They're sort of cute and homely," Earhart had told her husband laughingly. "They ought to be comfortable to wear under slacks for flying."

The article stressed that GP felt that he was literally the only person in the world who knew that fact. He declared that he was unable to find an explanation for Rothar's knowledge of that information:

"He still insists that no one knew that intimate little secret—and he would welcome a solution."

Still another small surprise was in store when I got to the very end of the article and read:

"Judge Freschi put this cold-blooded schemer away from the world for the rest of his natural life. And he will never torture a grieving man again. He is behind locked doors today, still the baffling, uncompromising man who made George Putnam's life an agony for three long days.

"Amelia Earhart is dead. So the courts of Los Angeles ruled in January 1939.

"And who can blame George Putnam for wondering and puzzling about the unanswered riddles in the fantasy of Wilber Rothar, the sailor who never went to sea."

This passage was surprising because Rothar's legal status at that time was that of a defendant undergoing evaluation to see if he was competent to stand trial for extortion. Moreover, the crime of extortion did not command a life sentence. When the *True Detective* article hit the newsstands, Rothar was languishing in a mental institution and not a jail. Admittedly, some of the discrepancies in that article may be due to artistic license on the part of the writer. However, the new spelling of the name, along with the additional details of the story, only increases the suspicion that the basic news story was completely bogus.

Yet another new piece of information in the article was a close-up photo of a nondescript looking man whom *True Detective* identified as Wilbur Rothar. (See earlier reproduction at beginning of article) The photo shows a middle-aged man, and not the "young man" of the Putnam family/Muriel Morrissey versions of the incident.

At first blush, Wilbur Rothar seems to be a man who knew "too much" and was silenced by being hustled off to a mental institution. This is supported by the fact that a level of knowledge was attributed to Rothar which only G. P. Putnam, by his own admission, possessed. If only Putnam knew those personal details, it was therefore most likely Putnam who supplied most of the scenario, which was recounted in the media. Given that fact, the fact that no one named Rothar ever existed, as well as the complete inconsistency of all recounts of the incident, the whole affair almost certainly seems to have been an elaborate ruse orchestrated by GP.

But why?

Going further, since everything that was publicized may have been fabricated, even the one "reality anchor" in the incident, the scarf belonging to Earhart, which was mentioned in news releases, may have been a fabrication too.

Unfortunately an, all too real, person was incarcerated in a mental institution.

Who was Wilbur Rothar?

The Psychic Side of
Amelia Earhart

There is an aspect of Amelia Earhart's life and disappearance of which most people are unaware. This aspect is almost more interesting than her aviation career and even her disappearance. For, aside from being the First Lady of Aviation, as she was dubbed, Amelia Earhart was also a considerable psychic.

Amelia Earhart ca 1929
(From author's collection)

Since she almost never discussed this side of her life publicly, information regarding it is scarce. However, I have uncovered some material which should be placed in this record and which the reader should find interesting.

The lead item in a column entitled "The Washington Merry-Go-Round" by legendary journalist Drew Pearson and his partner, Robert S. Allen, in the February 16, 1937 issue of the *Coshocton Tribune*, reported as follows:

"One development in connection with the recent air crashes which has been intriguing air officials is the way Amelia Earhart has gone psychic.

"America's foremost woman aviator has now become the No. 1 seeress of the air. She believes she has developed a contact with the occult world by which she knows what happens in air crashes.

"Her latest prediction is that May 10 she will make a startling discovery regarding the crash of the Western Air Express plane lost over the Wasatch Mountains on Dec. 15 between Salt Lake City and Los Angeles, and not yet located.

"Officials at first were inclined to laugh at Miss Earhart's psychic messages. But her accuracy now has them mystified. When a United Airlines plane was lost just outside of Burbank, Calif. Dec. 27, Miss Earhart called the United Airlines office and told them to look on a hill near Saugus, a little town north of Burbank.

"There the wreckage was found.

"Again when the Western Air Express plane carrying Mr. and Mrs. Martin Johnson crashed Jan. 12, Miss Earhart reported the plane to be near Newhall, 15 miles north of Burbank, where it was found.

"In the earlier crash of the Western Air Express in Utah, Miss Earhart had a vision to the effect that the bodies of the dead had been robbed by a trapper. Two days later, a trapper near Salt Lake City reported finding the wreckage, but then suddenly disappeared without giving the location of the plane.

"This is the unfound plane regarding which Miss Earhart expects to make a startling discovery on May 10."

Two days later in the Elyria Ohio *Chronicle-Telegram*, for February 18, 1937, an interview with Earhart in Cleveland was published. In part of the interview, she commented on the Drew Pearson column. Given the details of the Drew Pearson column, it was quite clear that Earhart was trying to completely downplay her psychic ability. That portion of the interview ran as follows:

"A few days ago a Washington columnist reported Washington agog over Amelia's 'psychic' ability to predict the location of lost planes. Commenting on the story today, Mrs. Putnam said:

'I suppose the story got started when I was searching north of Salt Lake City when all the others were searching south. The reason I went that way was not because I had been visited by spirits, but because that plane had a 50 mile tail wind and I reasoned it had been further along than the others thought.'"

A check of newspapers for later in the year, revealed news releases in June regarding the missing plane. The *Hammond Times* for June 8 reported on operations to remove the bodies of the crash victims and retrieve the mail and valuables from the wreckage. Evidently the craft had been discovered within the previous day or so, and interestingly, there was no mention of Amelia Earhart or the trapper who had reported the downed aircraft.

The two events are the only ones of Amelia Earhart's psychic ability to be found in the records so far. They seem to represent the only instances in which Amelia Earhart's psychic side was revealed.

It's understandable why Earhart would have all but debunked herself in the manner she did, as in a conservative era like the 1930s, a celebrity wouldn't want to be thought of as psychic. In those days, to be known as a psychic carried the risk of being thought of as a "kook", and Earhart's ambitions allowed no room for distractions such as this.

A remarkable article, entitled "Is Amelia Earhart Still Alive?" was published in the December 1939 and January 1940 issues of *Popular Aviation*. It described the communications from psychics received by GP, and also gave further hints regarding Earhart's own psychic side. The relevant portion ran:

"In looking back through the bright pages of Amelia Earhart's adventurous life, George Putnam remembered something that might explain the curious fervor of all those men and women who wanted to help in his hour of despair. It was simply that Amelia Earhart herself had a fragile psychic quality, some strange susceptibility to conditions beyond understanding. She rarely mentioned it to friends, never discussed it publicly. But whenever AE participated in mental telepathy or psychic experiments to further her curiosity, observers were astonished at the results. And yet she never involved or followed the advice of countless clairvoyants and astrologers who besieged her at every stage of her great flights.

"She used to say, laughing gaily:

"I haven't the courage to tell people my plans in advance. A pilot shouldn't worry and if I listened to every prediction I'd probably never leave the ground."

And, indeed, Earhart received profuse advice from psychics before her various flights. The feedback was usually in the form of warnings to her not to attempt her flight. And of course, each flight had been successful after all. That's probably the reason that, despite her knowledge of the reality of psychic phenomenon and her own psychic ability, Earhart disregarded all psychic warnings just before her round the world flight.

After Earhart's disappearance, psychics entered the picture again, via huge numbers of telegrams, letters and phone calls to GP. Commendably, he gave impartial consideration to every communication, even occasionally spending considerable sums to follow out promising leads.

Of all the strange communications that Putnam received after his wife's disappearance, the telegram he received on a late July morning at his Hollywood home, in 1937, may have been strangest. It ran:

"Amelia Earhart alive on coral shoal on one of Gilbert Islands latitude 2 above equator 174 longitude. This message received by Mr. L--- New York Medium."

An hour later, Putnam received a short note from a Captain T__ M__ of Cape Breton, Nova Scotia:

"...I am the retired captain of a copra boat that used to trade in the South Seas. I just happened to remember an uncharted island that we frequently visited for turtle eggs. The Gilbertese natives know where it is, too. The island is at—"

Here Putnam stopped in surprise and called his son David to locate the telegram he had received earlier that day. A few moments later, David returned with the telegram and the two compared the position given in that document with the position given in the note from Nova Scotia. Amazingly both positions were the same!

Putnam called the captain in Nova Scotia and the medium in New York for additional details. The details seemed sufficiently promising that the publisher immediately left for New York City, where two days later, he was able to arrange a check of the island by British authorities. A ship dispatched from Makin Island a short while later steamed for the location given in the two communications to GP. But eerily, there was no island at the given location. This baffled Captain M--- and his former crewmembers, who all swore they had visited the island a half a dozen times. The only explanation that could be put forth was that the island had suddenly been sunk by volcanic activity. GP spent $1000 on that adventure.

Probably the most famous psychic incident involved Jackie Cochran, one of Amelia Earhart's closest friends. After Earhart's disappearance, Cochran contacted GP, telling him that she had received strong psychic impressions that Earhart was floating at sea at a particular location east of Howland Island. Putnam practically moved heaven and earth to get the navy and coast guard to search that location. But the search was, unfortunately, fruitless, and Cochran later told Putnam that it was too late, that AE had perished.
Or had she?

Secret Cruises

Another side to the disappearance of Amelia Earhart, to which no attention at all has been given by other writers are several yacht cruises which took place between December 1937 and June 1940. Although they occurred well after the aviatrix' disappearance in July 1937, they are still of interest for what they reveal about the underlying political dynamics still apparent after Earhart's disappearance. They also indicate that the search for Amelia Earhart was still underway in the spring of 1940.

The first cruise involved a yacht called the *Athene*, which was owned by movie director Tay Garnett. Newspapers in late 1938 reported that he had outfitted his 105 foot boat with a complete photographic laboratory with the intention of going on an around-the-world cruise. The cruise was to allow Garnett to shoot scenic movie footage which would be used to spice up rear screen-projected backgrounds in a series of upcoming films.

Although the 1938 newspaper coverage of the cruise consistently indicated that the *Athene* left on its cruise in February 1938, I located a December 1937 newspaper with a photograph and long caption indicating that the boat was just about to leave on the voyage.

Interestingly, the write-up did not mention owner Tay Garnett, and the accompanying photograph showed George Palmer Putnam, movie actress Ione Reed, and the captain of the vessel. Another significant point is that the write-up mentioned only some locations in Mexico and Central America, and not the around the world trip touted in papers after the ship's return.

The voyage was reported to have ended in March 1938, at which time there was, oddly, little publicity.

Vincent Astor's yacht, the Nourmahal

Very interestingly, a cruise that did depart in February 1938 was that of the yacht *Nourmahal*, which was owned by multi-millionaire Vincent Astor. Astor was a good friend of FDR and also a member of FDR's informal network of amateur intelligence collectors (see Chapter 2, "Islands of Mystery"). From existing correspondence we know that the cruise traveled to the Central Pacific area, especially the Marshall Islands.

We also know that Astor was specifically sent by FDR on the cruise to seek out signs of a military buildup by the Japanese. He was to look for any bases, ports, airfields, or fueling facilities in the Marshall Islands and apprise FDR of their existence. At the conclusion of the cruise, Astor prepared and had hand-delivered a thirteen-page letter to FDR detailing his observations during the trip. What happened to that document is not clear, but researcher Ron Reuther located the following what follows undated note, circa spring 1938, in the FDR Library. Below is a transcription of it:

"Nourmahal

Dear Franklin:

Kermit has been with me on this whole cruise, and is leaving tomorrow at Honolulu to go back to work. He has had hardly anything to drink - and then only beer and sherry - and is in the best shape in years. When you see him, I think you will agree.

Vincent Astor

The information gathering side of our cruise has proved interesting, instructive, and, I hope will be helpful. On my return, I shall of course make a proper report to O.N.I. However, in the remote possibility of trouble between now and then, you might consider the following conclusions of mine concerning the Marshall Islands worth forwarding to Naval Operations & ON.I.

First. I did not visit any Japanese island. (Sounds fairly cowardly after the arrangements you made!) A letter received at Suva from the Jap Consulate General in N.Y. led me to believe that an application to visit their territory would be favourably considered. (This was probably a successful leg-pull on me). So I made my application through the N.Y. Consulate to the Minister of Overseas Affairs - Tokyo - to enter at Jaluit. Permission was withheld not only for this, but to go anywhere else in the Marshalls. (The radio correspondence is quite instructive).

I happened to have learned what happened to the two latest British Intelligence efforts, and it seemed evident that any attempt to get in would produce zero in useful results, and about a 100% probability of making serious trouble for you, & the State & Navy Depts. So I spent my time circulating amongst the neighboring Ellice & Gilbert Islands picking up all I could. Here are the results in Brief. They are not guaranteed as exact facts, but are conclusions which I believe to be substantially correct.

1. ENIWETOK, and not Jaluit or Wotje has been, and will be the principal naval base in these islands. A large dock with deep water alongside has been built on PARRY island. In 1935 some large naval units were observed in lagoon, the dock being then still under construction. Large fuel stores reported but on evidence which was not conclusive to me.

2. BIKINI. Probably their second string base, now being prepared. "Out of Bounds" to all visiting natives, and hence no information obtainable, except that supply ships are known to proceed there often.

3. WOTJE. There definitely is an airplane landing field (on the islet of Wotje) By March 1937, the space had been cleared of trees, and one or two houses (huts?) demolished. There is some evidence that a corner (or edge) of the lagoon is being filled in. Within last year 10 motor trucks (also tractors?) were landed. Apparently the cargo handling and pier facilities are very poor, and there is no evidence of their being improved. Lighters are used. In spite of this, 5000 tons of coal (Briguetttes) were landed last summer, slings from the lighters and manual power being used. (The trucks had a bad time.) Six (?) submarines & a tender have been observed in Wotje lagoon, the submarines always being alongside the ship when in port. There is a good fresh water supply from a fresh water pond about 2 acres in extent & 12 feet deep in center. The British impression is that Wotje will be used as a base for submarines, and Commerce raiders. (The coal suggests that too, re coal burning raiders). Some large concrete platforms have been constructed. As there is no evidence of guns, these might well be intended for warehouse floors. Some underground tanks are being dug; - the Japanese state for fresh water storage. However, as there appears to be a fairly ample natural water supply (from the pond) these might be intended for oil.

1. JALUIT I don't believe that there is much of military importance there, although the terminal of the air line to Ponape Etc. Jaluit is essentially the administrative seat of the islands, is the port of greatest commercial importance, and is the center of propaganda efforts. This last activity is quite a story in itself.

Fortifications. I feel moderately certain that there are none in the Marshalls.

Searchlights, and Observation balloons:- YES

Honolulu
We have just arrived. Please forgive the lack of continuity and the many failings of this report. I meant to improve it, but the ship has been overrun with everything from reporters to friends. (Plus Leis!)

I also hope I see you on getting home.

Affectionately and Respectfully.

Vincent"

--Obtained by Ron Reuther

On the surface it would appear to have been just another attempt by FDR to find out what the Japanese were up to in their mandated islands. But could there have been another even more covert reason? It is not impossible

The Yacht Yankee of Gloucester

that Astor was keeping a sharp eye out for Earhart, as he mentions in his letter to FDR that he had investigated the fate of two recent intelligence missions run by the British in the same area in which Earhart disappeared.

There are indications that G. P. Putnam had become frustrated with the navy's handling of the search for his missing wife. For another, the ship GP was reported to have left on for a "photographic cruise" had been, according to press releases the following year, ideally equipped for an espionage mission, with a state of the art photographic laboratory.

Overall, when one looks at the two overlapping cruise schedules of the ships and the ambivalent departure and return dates of the Athene, it becomes clear that there was probably more going on with these two ships than would casually appear.

A point is that there were at least three different reasons published for the cruise of the Athene. One was the collection of animals for the California Zoological Society, supposedly partially underwritten by G. P. Putnam. Another was the filming of a Tarzan-type film featuring Ms. Ione Reed in the title role of a female Tarzan. Yet another surfaced after the return of the Athene, and that was the filming of background footage in exotic locales to enhance a series of projected movies. Which was it? Just the fact that there were multiple published reasons for the trip raises suspicion of an intelligence gathering operation.

It has been speculated that GP may have left the *Athene* at a certain point in the cruise, very possibly the Galapagos Islands off the west coast of Ecuador. There, some researchers speculate, Putnam might later have been picked up by the *Nourmahal* before it steamed for the Marshalls, its published destination.

The above is at this point just a guess by some long-time researchers into Earhart's disappearance. However, the timing of the *Nourmahal*'s cruise seems far from pure chance, coming just months after Earhart's disappearance and in light of GP's impatience with the government's failure to locate his wife. Moreover, news releases indicated G. P. Putnam was listed as "leader" of the cruise of the *Athene* until it reached Mexico. There, Tay Garnett, the owner of the *Athene* was scheduled to join the vessel. These circumstances alone suggest there was another covert agenda afoot for the Athene.

What is known for sure is that Vincent Astor, who had at first been given the permission of the Japanese government to visit the Marshall Islands, was later denied entrance into the Marshalls shortly before he arrived in the area.

Astor, and possibly GP, had to be content to cruise the Gilbert and Ellice Islands. Whatever they may have found was never publicly revealed.

One more private cruise of interest occurred in April 1940. Although not secret, the endeavor was not extensively publicized. It was quietly organized by friends and associates of Earhart, who kept some of the key points of their future plan confidential. The organization, called the Amelia Earhart Foundation, was co-founded by former Earhart employee Elmer Dimity in 1938 and has for years remained in cryptic obscurity. After a brief flurry of publicity, during which the results of the cruise were never elaborated on at any length, the whole affair, including the organization that launched it, were little spoken of again. This is due in part to the fact that Purdue was already using the organization name at the time of the founding of the second foundation. A notable board member of the new foundation was Paul Mantz, who later withdrew. Moreover, the other members of the foundation, especially Mantz, were skittish about publicity, fearing that their search for Earhart would be misunderstood, although this writer cannot understand why. G.P. Putnam remained in the background so far his involvement with the foundation, as he was concerned about offending Purdue. Putnam made it clear that things should be kept low-key and businesslike, and it is clear that the rest of the foundation members followed this lead.

There was brief newspaper coverage beginning in the spring of 1940, with newspapers announcing in April that the Schooner Yankee, captained by Irving Johnson, was about to leave Honolulu for Samoa. According to the article, Johnson's mission was to make a preliminary search for Earhart and radio the results back to the Earhart Foundation for use in a future expedition.   Elmer Dimity was quoted as saying that the identity of the yacht to be used in the next expedition could not be revealed.

Dimity did go on to describe in some detail the characteristics of the vessel that would be used in the foundation's full-scale expedition. Provisioned for a one year cruise, the huge vessel would be capable of carrying six power boats and an amphibious airplane to aid in the search for the missing flyers. The announced skipper was Charles A. Watts, experienced in tropical waters.

Strangely, after this brief bit of coverage in April and early May 1940, there was no further mention of the expedition, and no published search results. Did they find anything? And if so, why didn't the Earhart Foundation share their results with the world?

Since none of these last ditch searches for the missing aviatrix yielded publicized results, we are left to wonder about them.   Are we being kept in the dark about what may have been found in the Central Pacific between the winter of 1938 and the summer of 1940? Or were all three searches abortive?

Amelia Earhart Philately

Amelia Earhart carried specially printed souvenir covers on all of her flights. Initially, they were carried in small quantities, strictly as souvenirs. During the 1928 Friendship Flight, for example, only three covers were carried, which were postmarked June 16, 1928 at Trepassey, Newfoundland and later on June 21, 1928 in London, England.

The number went up slightly with the 1932 solo flight across the Atlantic. On that flight, Earhart carried 50 covers, which bear a May 13, 1932 postmark in New York and a May 23, 1932 postmark in Londonderry, England. These were numbered and autographed.

On the 1935 Honolulu to Oakland flight, Earhart carried 49 numbered autographed covers. They were cancelled January 11, 1935 in Honolulu and January 12, 1935 in Oakland.

Courtesy of website for the National Postal Museum

On the 1935 flight to Mexico, Earhart carried 85 covers, 35 of which sported the 20 cent Mexican airmail stamp overprinted with "Amelia Earhart/vuelo/de bueno voluntad/Mexico/1935." This translated to "Good Will Flight 1935". Unfortunately, only several hundred were printed, two thirds of which were secured by G. P. Putnam. The philatelic world was not pleased when they learned how few of the stamps would be available to collectors. The 1935 overprint is now a highly sought, expensive philatelic item. Occasionally reproductions come up for sale on the Internet.

Courtesy of Bellarts Collection

Courtesy of website for the National Postal Museum

In 1936 the souvenir cover became a much more important financial factor, providing substantial funds for the round the world flight. Large quantities were sold and carried on the flight. They were sold through exclusive outlets negotiated by G. P. Putnam. The main outlet was the well-known and prestigious Gimbel's department store chain.

Ads would be placed in various newspapers and philatelic periodicals and order forms would be conspicuously available in each store to make it easy for customers to purchase covers when they were shopping. The ads stated that the covers would be canceled at Oakland at the beginning and end of the flight, as well as enroute either in India or Australia. Also, a Howland Island cachet, the first in history, would be placed on the covers.

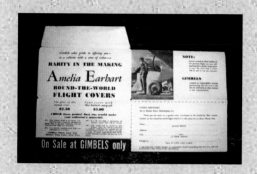

The price of the 1937 round the world flight cover was $2.50, or $5.00 if signed by Amelia Earhart. A monograph written by the late Archbishop Spelling reported that 10,000 covers were initially printed for the 1937 round the world flight. Of these, 6500 were sold and placed in the nose of Earhart's plane, before takeoff from Oakland to Honolulu on the first leg of the flight.

After the crash at Luke Field in March 1937, a second cachet was added to the covers reading, "Held over in Honolulu following Take-Off Accident of March 20, 1937." Another ad was placed by Gimbel's in philatelic periodicals in April 1937 indicating that a second cover was available for purchase for the second attempt at a world flight.

Above and below: front and back of a Gimbel's order form for an Around the World cover; Courtesy David Bellarts collection

By the time she took off from Oakland in May, an additional 1000 covers were sold and delivered to Amelia Earhart to place on her plane. The second cover was essentially the same as the first one in appearance, except that in the lower left corner there was stamped "2nd TAKE OFF" in a small black box. The only known surviving canceled cover from the first attempt at the round the world flight was one purchased by Mr. Elmer Dimity, who loaded the covers for the second takeoff on the Electra which Earhart received on May 28, 1937. After he had loaded the covers on the Electra, Mr. Dimity removed the one addressed to himself and placed it in his desk.

The only surviving covers from the second takeoff are those which Amelia Earhart gave to her mother before departing on the flight. A picture of one is shown in Muriel Earhart Morrissey's "My Courageous Sister."

In addition to the covers sold by Earhart's representatives, there were covers issued by various organizations and cities to commemorate various events in Earhart's career. These included covers to commemorate Earhart's visits to various cities, as well as the 1928 transatlantic flight, the fifth anniversary of the 1928 transatlantic flight, the 1932 transatlantic flight, the annual Cleveland Air Races, and various other aviation events. One of the most famous of these events was a route inaugurated in 1929 between Cleveland Ohio and Detroit, Michigan.

Personal Howland Island cover of RMC Leo Bellarts, with unique tinting; Courtesy David Bellarts collection

91

In the years since Earhart disappeared, there has been a continued if not increasing interest in them by philatelic collectors. The most famous collector of Earhart philately was Archbishop Spellman of the Catholic Church, whose collection is now on exhibit in the stamp museum named after him in Boston.

Since Earhart's disappearance, there have been many other covers issued to commemorate her career and her last flight. Probably the first cover after her disappearance was created on the USCGC ITASCA. According to Dave Bellarts, the ITASCA cover is probably the rarest Earhart cover in existence next to the second attempt round the world cover.

Only a few were made for ITASCA crew members, and a lot of these have since been lost. The cover shown in the illustration is the one bought by Chief Leo Bellarts. It is definitely a one-of-a-kind cover, as Chief Bellarts had hand colored the inner circles of the design in light blue and ended up bringing the cover home to his wife, since Earhart had not of course picked them up at Howland Island.

There seems to be a thriving market for Amelia Earhart philatelic items these days, especially on Internet auction sites.

From the author's collection, a commemorative cover Issued privately in 2007, featuring reproduced signatures of Amelia Earhart and Fred Noonan, as well as a cancellation at the Burbank Post Office. There are probably not too many of these in existence.

Above, an intriguing 4-stamp set issued by the Marshall Islands in 1987, commemorating the crash and rescue of Amelia Earhart.

Left, 75th Anniversary stamps issued recently by Palau; above, 50th anniversary stamp issued in 1987 by Mali; above right, souvenir sheet with one stamp issued recently by Tuvalu; Right, a four-stamp souvenir sheet issued by Tuvalu.

Bibliography

Books

ANDREW, Christopher, "For the President's Eyes Only: Secret Intelligence and the American Presidency from Washington to Bush", NY: Harper Collins Publishers, 1995

BRENNAN, T. C., "Witness to the Execution", CO: Renaissance House Publishers, 1988

BRIAND, Paul, "Daughter of the Sky", NY: Duell, Sloan and Pearce, 1960

BRINK, Randall, "Lost Star: The Search for Amelia Earhart", NY: W. W. Norton Co., 1993

CHAPMAN, Sally Putnam, "Whistled Like a Bird", NY: Warner Books, 1997

COCHRAN, Jacqueline, "The Stars at Noon", Boston: Little, Brown and Co. , 1954

DAVIDSON, Joe, "Amelia Earhart Returns from Saipan", Bloomington, IN: Unlimited Publishing,
2002

DEVINE, Thomas, with Richard D. Daley, "Eyewitness: The Amelia Earhart Incident", Frederick,
CO: Renaissance House, 1987

DEVINE, Thomas, with Mike Campbell, "With Our Own Eyes: Eyewitnesses to the Final Days of
Amelia Earhart", Lancaster, OH: Lucky Press, 2002

DONAHUE, James A., "The Earhart Disappearance: The British Connection", Terra Haute, IN:
Sunshine House, 1987

DWIGGINS, Don, "Hollywood Pilot: The Biography of Paul Mantz", Garden City, NY: Doubleday Co., Inc., 1967

EARHART, Amelia, "Last Flight", NY: Harcourt, Brace & Co., 1937

GOERNER, Fred, "The Search for Amelia Earhart", NY: Doubleday 1966

GOLDSTEIN, Donald M. and DILLON, Katherine V., "Amelia: A Life of the Aviation Legend" Washington, DC: Brassey's, 1997

KAHN, David, "The Code Breakers", NY: MacMillan, 1967, 9th Ed.

KENNEDY, Arthur with RIDLEY, Jo Ann, "High Times: Keep 'Em Flying", Santa Barbara, CA: Fithian Press, 1992

KING, Thomas, et. al., "Amelia Earhart's Shoes", Updated Edition, and Walnut Creek, CA: Alta Mira Press, 2004

KLAAS, Joe, "Amelia Earhart Lives", NY: McGraw Hill, 1970

KNAGGS, Oliver, "Amelia Earhart: Her Last Flight", Capetown, South Africa: Timmins Publishers, 1983

LONG, Elgen and Marie, "Amelia Earhart—The Mystery Solved", NY: Simon and Schuster, 1999

LOVELL, Mary, "The Sound Of Wings : The Life Of Amelia Earhart", NY: St. Martin's Press, 1992

MORRISSEY, Muriel, "Courage is the Price", Wichita, KS: McCormick-Armstrong Publishing Division, 1963

MORRISSEY, Muriel, and Osborne, Carol L., "Amelia, My Courageous Sister", Santa Clara, CA: Osborne Publisher, 1987

MYERS, Robert H., "Stand By to Die: The Disappearance, Rescue and Return of Amelia Earhart", Grove, CA: Lighthouse Writers' Guild, 1985

PELLEGRENO, Ann Holtgren, "World Flight", Ames, IA: Iowa State University Press, 1971

PERSICO, Joseph, "Roosevelt's Secret War", NY: Random House, 2001

PUTNAM, G. P. Jr., "Soaring Wings", NY: Harcourt, Brace & Co., 1939

RAFFORD, Paul Jr., "Amelia Earhart's Radio", Orange, CA 2006

Articles:

"A Woman Hops the Atlantic", <u>Literary Digest</u>, June 30, 1928

"Amelia Earhart: How Long a Mystery", <u>American Weekly</u>, September 10, 1944.

BRUDER, Jerry, "The Enduring Mystery of Amelia Earhart", <u>American History Illustrated</u>, May 1987

EARHART, Amelia, "Crossing the Atlantic", <u>American Magazine</u>, August 1932

DiTOMMASO, Lois; EMMONS, Sue and Kenyon, Donna, "Did Amelia Die or Was She Irene Bolam?", <u>Woodbridge NJ News Tribune</u>, October 18-29, 1982

GILLESPIE, Richard, "The Mystery of Amelia Earhart", <u>Life Magazine</u>, April 1992

JENNINGS, Dean S., "Is Amelia Earhart Still Alive?" <u>Popular Aviation</u>, December 1939 and January 1940

RILEY, John P., "The Earhart Tragedy: Old Mystery, New Hypothesis", John P. Riley, <u>Naval History Magazine</u>, August 2000

SOTHERN, Robert, "Trapping the Amelia Earhart Extortion Ghouls", *<u>True Detective Mysteries</u>*, January 1940

STATEN, Ron. "65 years later, the mystery of Amelia Earhart continues", AP, athens.com/stories/070202/new_29929702005.html.

"This Boston", <u>The Bostonian</u>, July 1928

Also:

Newspaperarchive.com

And:

Author's Collection

About The Author

David K. Bowman, USNR (Ret.)

David Bowman is also the author of three previous books, the award-winning LEGERDEMAIN, which was published by Saga Books in Canada, as well as THE FORGOTTEN STARS and TALES OF WESTPAC, through Amazon Kindle and CreateSpace.

LEGERDEMAIN placed as a Finalist in the 2008 National Best Books competition under History/U.S./Nonfiction. Dave is a member of the Amelia Earhart Society.

He is retired from the U.S. Naval Reserve, having served twenty-five years, two years of which were in the Vietnam War. He served on two cruises with VF-194 aboard the USS ORISKANY in 1969 and 1970.

Dave holds two degrees, one in accounting from Pacific Western College and one in general studies/archaeology from the University of Washington. He is also retired from a career of over thirty-one years with the State of Washington.

He makes his home in Auburn, WA.

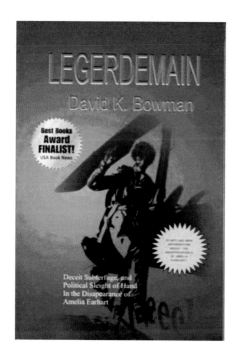

Find Out More About Amelia Earhart

LEGERDEMAIN is available through most book sites on the web and can be ordered through any book store. Also visit the following sites for more information:

www.sagabooks.net
www.davidkbowman.com

Price: $18.95
Published by Saga Books
474 pages

This award-winning book placed as a Finalist in the 2008 National Best Books competition and is the first book to bring together all the significant facts regarding the disappearance of Amelia Earhart in one volume. Earlier books have concentrated on a particular theory and have only presented a partial picture of the mystery.

Covered in LEGERDEMAIN are:

❑ The psychic abilities of Amelia Earhart
❑ The secret cruise of the Nourmahal
❑ Connection with the disappearance of the Hawaii Clipper
❑ The truth behind Paul Mantz' Electra
❑ The Putnam papers
❑ The bizarre mystery of Wilbur Rothar
❑ The cryptic telegram from George Huxford
❑ The startling account of Robert Myers
❑ The messages in a bottle found in Soulac-sur-Mer, France in 1938

LEGERDEMAIN also contains an exclusive new disclosure.

In addition, LEGERDEMAIN is profusely illustrated with footnotes, bibliography and numerous fact-filled appendices, making it a reference volume to be returned to for years.

Order your copy today!

Other books by David K. Bowman

Dave's story in words and vintage photos of two cruises to Southeast Asia (Western Pacific) in 1969-70 during the Vietnam War. Contains reproductions of five squadron newsletters full of photos and information about day to day life onboard the carrier USS ORISKANY. Available from Amazon Create Space in two editions, one with color illustrations and one with black & white illustrations. Also available as an eBook through Amazon Kindle. This one is a real walk down Memory Lane for the former carrier sailor or aviation squadron member.

A showcase of Dave's lifelong love of film, this book is the product of five years of research. Many of the biographical articles on old-time actors were published in magazines such as FILMFAX, CULT MOVIES, and SCARLET STREET. Some have never been published, although all of them are in their original versions. Available through Amazon Create Space in an economical printed version with black & white illustrations or a more expensive version with color illustrations. Also available through Amazon Kindle in a color illustrated eBook version.

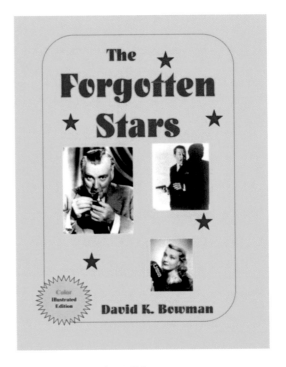

More information available at Dave's website at www.davidkbowman.com.

Made in the USA
Coppell, TX
05 December 2021

67114546R10067